PRAISE FOR TILL THE COWS COME HOME

'Lorna Sixsmith lovingly gathers together the stories and lore of place, home and family. Then she shines and polishes them to create pure gold.' – **Mairead Lavery, journalist with** *Irish Country Living* **and** *Farmers Journal*

'Lorna's deep-rooted attachment to the land … is woven into every sentence of this wonderful tale of a farming life … I found myself smiling from first page to last. Just wonderful.' – **Will Evans, host of** *Rock & Roll Farming* **podcast**

'Lorna Sixsmith intriguingly combines the roles of writer, historian, observer and participant in the unique way she captures so vividly the essence of daily life on her family farm for over a century.' – **PJ Cunningham, author of** *The Lie of the Land*

'An uplifting memoir with treasured stories and practical wisdom from a phenomenal author who successfully paints a powerful picture of farming life as a woman in agriculture.' – **Catherina Cunnane, journalist with** *That's Farming*

'Always humorous, Sixsmith is at her most passionate when describing how her unexpected inheritance of the family farm rekindled her connection with farming, strengthening her love of family past and present and sense of belonging to the land.' – **Mervyn Watson, former curator at the Ulster Folk and Transport Museum**

'This book is far more than a history of a family farm – it is a rich and detailed account of everyday life that will be of great interest to social historians.' – **Dr Ciara Meehan, Head of History, University of Hertfordshire**

'As a suburban dweller, I appreciated being introduced to many unknown aspects of farming life: the possible complications of calf births, the dietary demands of hired hands during silage season, the rich character traits of favoured cows. Lorna's retelling of all this and more makes for a very compelling read.' – **Louis Hemmings, poet and author**

'Lorna's style of writing is such that it transports you to the fields with her. A brilliant read, which I am sure I will return to again and again.' – **Emma Lander, 'Farmer's Wife and Mummy' blogger**

'An interesting, enjoyable, bucolic memoir about an Irish family and their farming history.' – **Suzanna Crampton, author of** *Bodacious: The Shepherd Cat*

'If you grew up on a farm, this book's attention to detail will breathe new life into the childhood sounds, sights, scents and simplicity that you once knew so well. A fabulously visual read.' – **Claire McCormack, journalist with** *AgriLand*

'A compelling account of one woman's love affair with her Irish farming heritage.' – **Debbie Young, author of the** *Sophie Sayers Village Mysteries* **series**

'Lorna believes in amusing her readers ... we have heard of things that would make a cat laugh. *Till the Cows Come Home* is enough to make a cow laugh!' – **Marjorie Quarton, author of** *Breakfast the Night Before*

'Sixsmith took me home and back to my childhood in the most beautiful way. A gem of a book.' – **Cat Hogan, author of the** *Irish Times* **bestseller** *There Was a Crooked Man*

LORNA SIXSMITH

Till the Cows Come Home

BLACK & WHITE PUBLISHING

To Brian, Will and Kate

First published 2018
by Black & White Publishing Ltd
Nautical House, 104 Commercial Street
Edinburgh EH6 6NF

1 3 5 7 9 10 8 6 4 2   18 19 20 21

ISBN: 978 1 78530 169 8

Two sections within this memoir are adapted from two short stories by
the author, published in anthologies edited by PJ Cunningham. 'The Travelling
Salesman' was published in *Then There Was Light* (Ballpoint Press, 2016).
'The Stranger in the Midst' was published in *Around the Farm Gate*
(Ballpoint Press, 2015).

A CIP catalogue record for this book is available from the British Library.

Typeset by Creative Link, Haddington
Printed and bound by CPI Group (UK) Ltd, Croydon, CR0 4YY

CONTENTS

GARRENDENNY FARM: A HISTORY

THE UNLIKELY FARMER

Garrendenny Farm has been home to the Sixsmiths for over one hundred years. When I left in 1987 to spread my wings, I never imagined myself back here, let alone farming. Yet, in July 2005, there I was, gasping for breath in the middle of a field trying to catch a runaway calf. 'Can you not run faster?' I heard Brian shout as I tried, in vain, to stop the calf. She raced past me, ignoring my waving arms. She slowed down a hundred yards from us but still watched us carefully. Her head and tail were raised high, signifying she was ready to gallop again. I stopped to draw breath.

It was coming up to our third farming anniversary. We had just moved into the farmhouse and here we were on a Sunday morning, trying to retrieve a four-month-old calf from a neighbour's field. Eighty calves had been put into Peter's Field the previous day and, when herding them that morning, Brian noticed one was missing. Somehow, calf number 1342 had squeezed through the hedge and into a neighbour's field. It was a large field divided into paddocks by electric wire; yearling Charlaois cattle viewed us with some curiosity from one of them. The last thing we wanted was the calf getting in with them or running through another hedge into a further field. It would be impossible to retrieve her if that happened so we absolutely had to get her back.

This was the third time we had tried to run her towards a corner, hoping that her brain would register it would be a good idea to squeeze back through the now enlarged gap in the hedge and rejoin her friends. So far it hadn't worked. It wasn't easy to round up a single calf – and this one was too flighty, too skittish, too fast. She had probably been stung by the electric wire too and was scared of it happening again.

'We'll try again,' said Brian with the look of a man who was going to die trying. And I could tell Dad was just about to say, 'It'll never work,' when Brian went marching off again in pursuit of the runaway.

For a split second, I allowed myself to remember my pre-farming life. Sunday mornings were usually devoted to decorating or reading the newspapers over a leisurely breakfast. Even sanding architraves would be more relaxing than this. We used to reward our efforts with a pub lunch or a picnic in the New Forest, followed by a leisurely stroll for a couple of hours. I groaned as I started to jog after Brian. I wasn't fit; it was about four years since my last aerobics class. I wasn't wearing a sports bra, my jeans were belt-less and kept slipping down and the ground was so rough I was convinced I'd break or sprain an ankle if I didn't watch my step. I didn't respond well to shouts from my husband to run faster either. I wasn't cut out to be a farmer at all.

We created a semicircle around the calf, each of us holding

out a stick to elongate our arms and try to create a barrier, and in this way we closed in on her slowly. Thankfully she took the hint and walked in the right direction as we whispered encouragement to her. We got closer this time; at last she was going towards the corner. We had enlarged the gap she had escaped through, and we had to just cross our fingers that she would go back through it. The other calves were at the other side of the hedge now, maybe their presence would encourage her. She walked closer and closer as we closed in tighter and tighter. She seemed to be concentrating on the other calves now rather than being wary of us. She climbed up the small incline and Brian raced forward to push her on further. We'd done it.

Calf number 1342 spent the rest of that summer with her comrades on the outfarm as I started to adjust to rural life, helping out at fundraisers, cooking for contractors and getting to know the neighbours. Two years later, as she had her first calf and entered the milking herd, our eldest child started primary school and I got a position on the school's board of management. Was I starting to settle in to rural farming life after years of being a city girl?

Growing up as a farmer's daughter, I developed a love for the land yet never saw myself becoming a farmer. In Ireland, as in many other countries, farms traditionally passed down the male line. My brother, Alden, was nine years younger than me. I just assumed he would take on the family farm. My extensive list of allergies – to dust mites, dairy products, grass pollens, straw and many other things – probably further indicated that farming wasn't the best career choice. And I wanted to emigrate, to experience life outside of Crettyard, of Dublin and of Ireland. I didn't want to marry a farmer, not because of the hard work and long hours, but because I'd have to live in the same place for decades. I wanted to spread my wings.

Yet, here I was back in Crettyard, destined to live in the same house for the next quarter of a century. Accustomed to renovating a house every two years and moving on, I sensed I'd be moving the furniture around frequently.

It's true that the tie to the family farm is usually very strong because it has been passed down from generation to generation. No one wants to be the generation to sell that land. It's a fact that farms in Ireland don't come on the market as often as in other countries. Land exchanges hands once every four hundred years in Ireland compared to every seventy years in France. I was aware that the responsibility to be a good farmer and hand the farm on to the next generation in an improved state can be a challenge. Could I relish the challenge of being self-employed, loving farm life and being at one with nature? Would it be a dream career and an ideal lifestyle? I had a love for the land, yet would it become a millstone around my neck? Would I feel too tied down by it? Time would tell.

I'm the fourth generation of Sixsmiths to farm at Garrendenny. Looking back at my ancestors, not all were interested in farming. To the best of our knowledge, the first of my ancestors to come to live in this part of Ireland, a Joseph Sixsmith, was from Yorkshire, an engineer specialising in open cast mining. Many local families, including the Wandesfordes, the local estate owners who held mining rights for centuries, came from Yorkshire in the seventeenth and eighteenth centuries. My great-uncle Charlie, an eldest son, was more interested in engineering and mechanics than farming. Some of my father's cousins had careers in restoring steam engines and cryogenics engineering. Our son Will looks to be following in those engineering footsteps, as his favourite subjects are physics and maths.

Who were the Sixsmith farmers? My great grandfather Joseph was a farmer and builder, his second son George, my grandfather, became a farmer. Dad was a second son and inherited the home farm. He was interested in dairy farming whereas his older brother Georgie wanted to grow arable crops.

But was farming Dad's first choice of career? He was reasonably bright in primary school. His eldest sister had been tutored by her grandmother and won a scholarship to a boarding school. His grandfather was determined to succeed with one of the younger children and used to take great delight in showing off to visitors with Dad's ability to spell and do mental arithmetic. His teacher wanted him to try for a scholarship, but his parents weren't so keen. They probably considered it a better use of a fourteen-year-old's time for him to stay at home and milk cows than to go away to boarding school. Initially Dad didn't mind – until he was on his hands and knees weeding sugar beet on cold, wet days. Boarding school and study looked a much more attractive prospect then. My dad has always loved farming, though. At almost eighty years of age, he still potters around and has an interest in any births, changes and improvements on the farm.

How did I end up farming? I inherited the farm because my younger brother Alden decided farming wasn't for him. I always felt that was a brave decision; many people opt to farm because they feel it is expected of them not because it suits them. Farming is a wonderful life, but it's tough, and demanding and very particular in what it asks of you. It is not for everyone.

My husband Brian and I had been living in Salisbury in England for almost twelve years. I was a secondary school teacher, and he was a scientist. Our hobby was renovating and decorating houses. Like me, Brian had been brought up on a farm but, as a second son, he knew he wouldn't inherit and so went to college. We'd always joked that dairy cows are his first love, so when Dad didn't want to sell or lease the farm and offered it to us, we spent a lot of time mulling it over.

It was a huge decision. We'd be giving up so much – our careers, our pensionable jobs, weekends off, paid annual leave. I enjoyed living in Salisbury; it's a beautiful city. I loved, too, the anonymity of living in England. No one knew when we took risks buying a house. No one cared when I went back to university at the age of twenty-four. Relatives didn't know we camped out in a house while we made it habitable. We weren't talked about or commented on – well, not to the best of my knowledge. We'd be coming back to a community where the smallest things we did on the farm would be analysed and cogitated over, where people would see fit to let us know their thoughts on all that we did. We were both aware of the long hours demanded by farming. Could I, a person who wasn't keen on cooking, who wasn't a great housekeeper, who valued my own privacy ... could I become a farm wife? Could I live in a small, rural community where everyone knows everything about everyone? Would I be able to milk cows and feed calves unaffected by my allergies? Would we be able to live on a farm income and still enjoy a decent standard of life? Would I be capable of becoming a person who arranges flowers for church, has tips for curing ailments and can get rid of difficult stains? Could I be strong if things went badly wrong, such as a severe loss of livestock? Might I be lonely? Would we be able to give our children an idyllic childhood similar to the one I had experienced and would they thank us for it?

Yet, we hankered to be self-employed, to work in a business that could flourish by our own efforts, to be our own boss, to work with animals and the soil, and for our children to have a country childhood. We thought about how our children would get to know their grandparents, cousins and other family members properly – living alongside them and participating in the fabric of their lives. We were already clear that our future plans included an aim to live on a smallholding in Devon, Yorkshire or France in any case.

And so, for better or worse, we moved back to Garrendenny in July 2002. At the time, Will, our first-born, was three weeks old. The farm was legally transferred the following year.

As we work in the same fields that my forebears ploughed, as our cows graze the same fields that their ancestors grazed, as we make changes and improvements, there is a feeling of continuing the heritage of farming here. As we acknowledge and remember the efforts of those who went before us, we are aware that we can't control the future of the farm once we retire. We are custodians of this farm just as our predecessors were. It is our responsibility to farm it well, to enjoy the journey, to earn a decent living from it, and to move with the times so that the farm is a viable business. Then it will be ready to hand on to the next generation should they choose to be farmers too.

WHERE IS GARRENDENNY?

Garrendenny is a small townland tucked away in a tiny corner of County Laois, in the south-east of Ireland. It is a quiet part of the world now, but once it was within a few miles of one of the most densely populated rural areas in Ireland. In 1832 it was claimed the area contained more people than any city in the country, except Dublin and Cork. The coalmines provided employment for thousands of people and as the wages they offered were better than those paid for farm labour, people came to this area in search of work. Cabins were thrown up along roadsides and villages grew at intersections. It was once a very lively place to live and has achieved notoriety on more than one occasion. The village of Crettyard is less than a mile from the farm at Garrendenny and has two shops and a creamery (agricultural store). The nearest small town is Castlecomer, five miles away, which is now well resourced with schools, a bank, supermarkets, cafés, a library, craft shops and the Discovery Park with its woodland walks, lakes and museum. Thus, Garrendenny has the best of both worlds – perfect solitude and yet only minutes from civilisation.

THE BUTLER FAMILY OF GARRENDENNY

From 1708 the original estate at Garrendenny was owned by a branch of the Ormond Butlers. Its eight hundred acres weren't exactly prime agricultural land with stunning parklands and landscaped lawns – old records note the prevalence of 'shrubby wood, bog and decayed timber'. But still, Garrendenny did boast a castle, albeit a very small one.

In 1795 Edmund Theobald Mandeville Butler, the owner of Garrendenny, inherited the right to the title of Viscount

Galmoy. Neither Edmund Butler nor his son, Piers Theobald, pursued the claim. When Piers died unmarried in 1824, his younger brother Garrett took it upon himself to assume the title, and locals still occasionally refer to the gateway to the farm as 'the Lord's Gate'. In those times, most landlords were absentee, but, unusually, Garrett lived at Garrendenny.

By all accounts, Lord Garrett Butler led a rather scandalous life. He married in 1835, but it is believed his wife, Mary Ryan, died in childbirth. She and her baby were buried in the nearby graveyard in Kilgorey and Garrett hired local men to guard the grave for a few days in case their bodies were stolen by grave robbers. He married seventeen-year-old Ellen Burke in December 1840, a mere three weeks after meeting her, having convinced her of his wealth. His estate at the time was worth £1,500 a year. Ellen was noted to be beautiful with a 'ruddy complexion, dark eyes, good skin and sandy hair'. While she was at Garrendenny, raucous parties were held in the drawing room and much alcohol was consumed. Things sometimes got out of hand. On one occasion, visitors, servants and Ellen ran from the castle to shelter in nearby trees, as Garrett allegedly shot over their heads with his rifle. However, Ellen didn't stay at Garrendenny for long. Divorce proceedings were undertaken in 1844, but each application failed when Ellen and Garrett were both shown up to be adulterers. They created quite a scandal at the time, judging by the newspaper reports, and an outraged judge said he hoped 'that his court might never again be polluted by the hearing of such infamous proceedings as the evidence had disclosed.'[1] In 1841, a baby baptised in the nearby church was described as the illegitimate daughter of Garrett Butler and Eliza Frizell, spinster of Mayo (the adjoining townland to Garrendenny). By 1849, Garrett had four daughters – Elizabeth, Anne, Geraldine and Isabella – and two sons, Edmund Fitzgarrett and Pierce. His children were impoverished compared to other gentry. According to family letters, they felt they hadn't sufficient means to carry their rank properly. Locally, the boys were viewed as young lords and the girls as ladies but their illegitimate status would have raised eyebrows in society. Edmund Fitzgarrett Butler was admitted as a member of the Royal College of Surgeons in 1871, and the daughters emigrated to New Zealand and Canada.

Garrett Butler died on 28 March 1860 aged sixty, and is buried in Mayo church, where the slab marking his grave records him as the ninth Viscount Galmoy. Despite the scandals, it seems he was well liked by locals. A local newspaper reporting on Garrett's death wrote, 'Although a man of eccentric character, he was possessed of a high order of intelligence'.[2]

THE WARRENS – THE LAST OF THE LANDLORDS

In 1876 Hubert Warren became the new owner of Garrendenny. He soon acquired a reputation for being a harsh landlord – he didn't hesitate to evict tenants, some for the non-payment of rent, but also because he wanted to use the land for his own crops and livestock.

However, when the Land Act of 1903 was passed, Warren sold 726 acres to existing tenants. He got married in 1904. Huge celebrations were held at Garrendenny. The castle and grounds were decorated, bonfires blazed and there was dancing on the lawns. A few months later, he sold the rest of the estate and moved to Canada. An advert in a local paper listed the following items for sale: fifty Aberdeen Angus and Shorthorn-cross cattle, five young cows, five springers, twenty cheviot ewes and lambs, and twenty-one horses.

A NEW ERA FOR GARRENDENNY

Joseph Sixsmith (born 1836, died 1920), worked as a steward for a local landlord and was granted some land. His son, Herbert, my great grand-uncle inherited one hundred acres at Doonane (now part of our farm, but located two miles away from Garrendenny), and he purchased eighty acres at Garrendenny in 1906. Not much is remembered of Herbert although he seems to have been a very matter-of-fact man who was popular in the area. He was charmingly described as being 'as decent a man as was ever shod in shoe leather' in a local history.[3] Interestingly though, local newspaper reports indicate that he got in trouble with the authorities for not growing the stipulated amount of grain during the First World War. Herbert died childless in 1939, and when his wife Rebecca died in 1945, the farm was left to my grandfather George Sixsmith (Herbert's nephew), and the whole family moved here.

Herbert's brother, Joseph, was my great-grandfather. He owned a small farm near Doonane and also worked as a builder. He met Malahath Boveniser from Limerick, when she was working as a governess locally. The Bovenisers originally came to Ireland from Germany, fleeing religious persecution. Joseph and Malahath soon married, going on to have two sons and two daughters. They sold their small farm and bought a much larger one with a fine house. But Joseph wasn't as fortunate in his business dealings as Herbert and times were hard during the late 1920s. As money tightened, the situation worsened, so the bank sold the farm. The couple then rented a farm for a few years before buying a hundred acres in Ballybrommel, near Carlow.

Joseph was viewed as somewhat eccentric. When his daughters got married, he didn't attend the weddings as he said 'he hadn't reared his daughters to give them away to any man'. Was he a feminist or did he just hate all the fuss of a day out? After losing the farm to the bank, he handed all business decisions over to his son George, never dealing with banks or any financial matters and refusing to draw his pension when he became eligible. I am told that he was an extremely fussy eater, telling my grandmother off if she served meat with a sliver of fat to any of her children, and never eating eggs or custard because of his aversion to the colour yellow.

NEW BEGINNINGS

It was 1946 when the family comprising of my great-grandfather Joseph (Malahath had died in 1941), my grandparents George and Lily, and their children moved to Garrendenny. They soon settled in, with neighbours calling in to say hello and the children cycling to the primary school three miles away. The fact that George had a car and they had bicycles, however rickety they might have been, meant they were viewed as relatively well off by some. We forget just how tough circumstances could be for some people in those days. They probably were affluent when compared to the neighbour who brought piglets to the fair in the 1930s, and who had to drown them on his return when he couldn't find a buyer. He couldn't afford to feed them.

My grandfather George was a man of ritual. He was a

quiet man, and on a Sunday evening he would sit in the kitchen smoking and chatting to his brother Charlie, while his wife's clan conversed in the sitting room. In the summer Charlie usually called up on Wednesday evenings and the two of them would sit out in the field in front of the house, watching the sun go down and the world go by.

George didn't do many jobs in the house, but his one task was to lift the potatoes out of the cooking pot and onto people's plates and the central serving dish. His fingers were so hardened by years of smoking that the heat of the potatoes didn't affect him at all.

Every Thursday, without fail, no matter if hay needed to be saved or corn needed to be cut, George went grocery shopping. He drove to Dublin Street in Carlow and left the shopping list in the grocery shop. He then went to visit Charlie in his radio shop, and sat chatting and smoking while Charlie worked on fixing a radio. George then returned to the grocer's to collect his shopping and drove home, arriving in time for tea when all the yardwork was done. He would also drive to Castlecomer on Saturdays to buy meat for the following day's dinner, and would take the children to church on Sunday mornings.

George died, aged 61, in 1964, the year before my parents got married. My father inherited the farm that year.

GARRENDENNY LANE

We live less than a mile from the village of Crettyard. In many ways, it hasn't changed much in half a century. It still has two shops, one of which includes a post office, and a creamery (an agricultural store). Connor's pub closed in the 1980s, the nearest public house now being two miles in the direction of Carlow. There are two churches and a primary school within a mile of the village. Within two miles of Crettyard are impressive sports facilities for a rural area: a football pitch, a handball alley and a very popular athletics club.

The full length of Garrendenny Lane is one and a half miles. It runs from Kilgorey, a rural area of green fields, bogs, quarries, coalmines and cottages, spanning 363 acres, down to the townland of Mayo where the two schools and two churches were daily and weekly destinations respectively for local dwellers. The lane bordered the farm in my grandfather's day, but as Dad, and then we, purchased more land in 1996 and 2007, the lane now divides the farm and we travel along it most days.

It is quiet now, but was a busy thoroughfare until the 1970s. Children from Kilgorey walked to school in Mayo along the lane. They left a little pile of stones in a specific place to signal to latecomers that they had gone on and wouldn't be waiting for them. On the way home during the autumn, the children ate blackberries and crab apples, occasionally calling into one of the cottages and getting a slice of bread and butter. On Sundays, families walked along the lane to Mass. At night, people rambled in the dark and visited other houses to exchange news, play cards and swap stories. Cattle ambled along when being moved from one field to another, grazing along the ditches.

Before 1900, there were many cottages along the lane, the homes of tenant farmers. Most of these rented one or two fields, grew potatoes and oats, reared a pig to pay the rent, and some had a couple of cows or goats. Smoke furled from chimneys, candles twinkled in tiny sash windows and voices rumbled by firesides. The homesteads steadily reduced in number after the evictions of the 1880s. These evictions were unfortunately common as many landlords wanted to get rid of tenants so they could farm the land themselves. After the Land Acts of the early twentieth century, any remaining tenants were able to purchase land. There were only three dwellings left along the lane by the 1960s, all inhabited by spinsters and bachelors. This wasn't unusual as the marriage rate in Ireland was low in the mid-1900s, but it meant that they relied on neighbours for camaraderie and companionship.

One such bachelor was Jack Bolger, who lived on his own in a two-storey farmhouse until 1981. Farming a hundred acres (of which we now own sixty-four), he fattened cattle, borrowing a tractor from his brothers when he needed one. He lived a solitary life, sharing his kitchen with young calves that he penned in on the other side of the dresser. He sourced his water from a sunken well in the field, lowering a bucket using a rope and hauling it up again. Likewise, another bachelor, Jimmy Lynup lived in a one-room cottage with small extensions at either end for housing calves and for storage. The Wade family, consisting of a sister and two brothers, lived in a two-bedroom cottage. It sold recently, but as no one is living in it as yet, I still call in occasionally. The only items left in the cottage are the range cooker and the cast iron fireplaces, but it still feels like a happy place as I look out the tiny windows across open fields down to the main road. The large flagstones on the kitchen floor are still in place and the bedroom floors are concreted, one with a love heart marked into it with the date 1924.

As dwellers died and weren't replaced by a younger

generation, the use of the lane declined. The road surface was never tarred so it was unsuitable for cars. People drove the longer route by the main road instead. Very few people walk or drive along it now, although on the rare occasion that we block it with the loader when moving cattle, we have sometimes returned to see someone sitting there in their jeep or tractor waiting patiently.

The lane is narrow with high hedges, much higher than they were years ago. For the most part, the road is grown over with grass in the centre. Some stretches feel quiet and enclosed; other parts open up with views for miles. As it meanders and undulates, there's a lovely sense of peace and solitude. I particularly like the sections where I can see the whole long line of cows ambling along in front of me. It gives me the sense that cows have done this for centuries.

In May, the lane is lush with long grasses and bluebells in the ditches. The summer brings honeysuckle and blackberries, and everything dies back in the winter as the ice-covered puddles crunch and split under my feet. As I walk along, listening to the birdsong and often in a world of my own, it feels like the friendly ghosts of cows and people from a bygone age still linger there.

2

FARMING THROUGH THE GENERATIONS

MIXED FARMING

Most farms in the 1940s had a mixture of enterprises and Garrendenny was no different. They had cows, cattle, sheep, pigs, poultry, corn, sugar beet, vegetables and potatoes. The spread of enterprises meant there was a stream of income throughout the year and they were largely self-sufficient for essential foodstuffs. During the Second World War (the 'Emergency' as it was known in Ireland), owing to the shortage of grain, all farms in Ireland had to grow wheat, oats or barley under the Compulsory Tillage Order. They were urged to plough and till more land with demands for more and more wheat. The percentage required increased as the war went on. If farmers didn't comply, their lands could be confiscated. Like most farm families, Sixsmiths sold the wheat and kept their barley and oats for their own livestock to eat.

Farming was much more labour intensive then. Families tended to be large and as soon as they were old enough to be useful, children helped on the farm or with the housework.

The three Sixsmith boys fed calves, carried water, fed pigs, chopped sticks for the fire, stood in gaps to stop animals escaping and, as they got older, milked cows and worked in the fields. The six girls carried water and helped with housework and cooking. All of this was done without question or complaint. My grandfather George was often described as delicate. He didn't work too hard. He was about five foot six tall, of slight build, a heavy smoker and had heart problems from his early fifties. When my great grandfather became too old to plough, George employed a ploughman. This was a role that held more status than other farm jobs such as yardman or milker. And this status reflected the skills required to plough a good straight furrow and care for the horses. Pat Patterson got the job and stayed with the Sixsmiths for nearly twenty years. As he was the only workman, he did other tasks too, such as milking cows and droving cattle. There wasn't enough room for Pat to sleep in the house, so Joseph, having worked in the building trade as well as farming, built him a bedroom adjoining the house in Ballybrommel. Later, Pat moved to Garrendenny Castle with the family and slept in one of the bedrooms on the top floor.

The supply of milk from the fourteen Shorthorn cows to the creamery delivered a monthly milk cheque. At that time, the milk was separated at the creamery; they kept the cream and the farmers took the skimmed milk home again. There, it was mixed with barley and fed to the pigs. The farm's eight sows had two litters a year, producing up to fourteen piglets per litter. Once weaned, they were fattened in numbers of approximately twenty in each shed. There was also a small number of sheep, a maximum of thirty at any one time.

Chickens varied in number; the females provided eggs and the males went into the cooking pot.

Eggs were scarce in the winter, as hens laid fewer eggs in the cold frosty months. This meant that it was more expensive to buy fresh eggs at this time of year, so my grandmother Lily preserved eggs when they were plentiful during the summer. The eggs were coated in soft butter and stored in an enamel bucket filled with cold water and waterglass (another name for sodium silicate). Preserved eggs were used for baking and customers were glad of them in the run-up to Christmas. They sold for a lower price than fresh eggs in the winter but fetched more than if sold as fresh eggs during the summer months.

The Sixsmiths had two turkey hens and a turkey cock, so every year about thirty turkeys were fattened for Christmas. Most were sold, while the remainder were for gifts and the family's own consumption. Another way to make money was to charge for the breeding services of the male. Neighbours would bring their own turkey hens to visit him, transporting their turkeys in baskets on old black bicycles, by ass and cart or occasionally in a tractor. My mother-in-law used to take their turkey hen off to visit a turkey cock, bringing her in the basket on her bicycle as she cycled the two miles there and back.

'Well, that just proves I married up,' Brian said one day when we were exchanging 'turkey' stories. 'Your ancestors had their own cockerel.'

The importance of the potato in the Irish diet has been well documented in reports since the Great Famine. This was because potatoes could sustain a family and were the main foodstuff for many dwellers on small plots of land.

The Sixsmiths planted an Irish acre of potatoes every year

(equal to 1.6 English acres). They were mostly Kerr's Pinks, with a few drills of Golden Wonders, which were better for eating later in the year, and a few drills of British Queens for early potatoes. The boys and Pat sowed the potatoes every April, which involved Pat opening up the drills with the horses and a two-sod plough. They all shared the job of spronging dung before walking along the drills planting the potatoes from the piles within the half-sacks tied to their waists. Pat then had the task of splitting the drill once again to send earth down on top of the potatoes. It wasn't as easy as it looked; he had to ensure the horses walked along the earth of the drill rather than on the potatoes.

All the children had a week off school in October to pick potatoes and felt as rich as kings at the end of the week when they each received the princely 'wages' of ten shillings. There was a potato digger, pulled by the two horses, which lifted the clay and then the spinner threw out the potatoes. Pat drove the horses and they would pick all the potatoes in one drill before digging the next one. Everyone had their own two-handled potato basket and, once filled, it was carried to the pit in the field. My grandfather, George, dug three or four pits in the field. They were about three feet wide, six inches deep and of varying lengths. The children and Pat would pile up the potatoes, while George was the 'pit steward', who supervised the building of the pile. When finished, it was covered with straw and then clay to protect the potatoes. Potatoes to be eaten in the next few weeks were put into the dark, cold potato shed in the yard.

In the spring, the potatoes from the pit were brought to the potato shed and George indulged in one of his favourite jobs. He only sold potatoes at this time of year. He sorted through the potatoes and was very particular; he wouldn't let a bad potato go into a bag. Locals came up with their asses and carts and took away one or two sacks of seed potatoes for planting their own plots. He also sold bags of eating potatoes, and every second year he bought in seed potatoes certified by the Department of Agriculture.

Considerable importance was attached to the quality and quantity of the potato harvest. 'How are the spuds with you?' was a frequent question when in conversation with neighbours. The replies varied. They might be only tiny 'skillauns' under the stalks, or, if the harvest looked promising, 'the ground was white with them'. If they weren't of great quality you could 'stick them to the wall', but the highest regard was awarded to potatoes that were 'balls of flour'. Even now, 'floury' potatoes are our favourites. Any potatoes that crack open when boiled in their skins are still considered the best. I often hear talk revolving around where to get the flouriest potatoes, and if a supplier's potatoes are a disappointment they'll hear all about it.

My grandparents also grew turnips in the fields and vegetables in the garden. They never planted carrots, as they didn't like them, but planted rhubarb, cabbage, onions, peas, lettuce and parsnips. Cooking and eating apples were handpicked and were carefully placed in layers in barrels, with fine sand separating them so that they would last until March or April. Neighbours called up every autumn to get a few bags of apples and sometimes Lily gave the children a few pears too.

THE FIRST TRACTOR AND TRAILER
My grandparents had two Shire horses when they moved

to Garrendenny in 1946. It was hard to get good working horses then. Peggy and Dolly were treasured; both were very strong. Dolly trotted to keep up with Peggy's long stride and they worked well together. The horses were fed on the best of the hay – always the first crop – and oats. They were let out to graze at night and were fed oats when the workers were having their dinner. They consumed enough oats within that hour to give them energy for the rest of the day's work.

Peggy was the best horse they ever had. She marched up and down the field ploughing straight furrows and once she'd had a rub down, food, water and a sleep, she was raring to go again the next morning. But in 1954 she dropped dead in the yard. Some said it was a twisted gut. George suspected a heart attack, as it happened so quickly. Nonetheless, they needed another horse, so George and his eldest son Georgie tried to find one to purchase. They couldn't find a horse as big or as strong as Peggy, who my grandfather said was capable of 'pulling a house'. How was she going to be replaced?

In the end they discovered a tractor wasn't much more expensive than a large Shire horse and decided to purchase a grey Ferguson TE20 for £400. They also purchased a non-tipping trailer for £96. They could have spent another £25 and bought a tipping trailer but, for the sake of economy, must have decided that forking the contents off the trailer would be easy enough work. As it turned out, manually loading and unloading the trailer of hay, dung, turnips, beet or stones was more time-consuming and backbreaking than they had anticipated. This non-tipping trailer was sworn at many times during its lifetime. It wasn't long before the extra £25 seemed small money. What's more, the process of starting up and driving the tractor had to be learned.

Tractor vaporising oil (TVO) was the fuel used, but when the tractor was cold it had to be started up with petrol. Once it had heated and was moving, the operator switched the fuel source back to TVO. A similar process was followed before it was switched off. George never really got the hang of it. He was in his fifties and still hankered after the horses: starting up the tractor was so much more complicated than an easy 'gee up' or 'whoa'.

However, the tractor meant more opportunities for making money. When they purchased a mowing bar, many small farmers and those with cottage plots of half an acre hired the Sixsmith boys to mow their meadows to save them time and energy – as previously they had cut the grass by hand with a scythe. Georgie went out in the evenings with the tractor and mowing bar, charging his neighbours £1 per acre of land mowed, while Joe – who of course became my dad – stayed at home and milked the cows. 'There was no money in milking cows,' he would say ruefully.

The tractor meant some farming practices changed. Certainly, ploughing was faster with a tractor than the Shire horses – tractors didn't get tired, whereas the horses had to be rested. The Compulsory Tillage Order had ended and most fields were in grass, but now the Sixsmiths decided to grow more corn. The brothers differed in their approach to ploughing. For the first furrow in a field, Georgie insisted on pushing pegs into the ground and having a sibling stand at the opposite hedge to ensure he ploughed a meticulously straight furrow. Dad simply fixed his eyes on something directly opposite him in the far ditch, be it a tree or a bush, and drove straight towards it. Which would I do? I know I'd opt for the latter, but I doubt I'd achieve the straight furrow.

The Ferguson TE20 was traded in by 1958 for the diesel-fuelled Massey Ferguson 38, about which there was a huge buzz in the farming world. My family, like many others, found it to be a huge improvement.

TEAMWORK IN FARMING

Up to the mid-twentieth century, it was rare for women to plough fields, even if they did other work with horses or worked in the fields tying sheaves or turning hay. My grandfather George ploughed, tilled and harvested the crops with their workman Pat. He would help with milking cows, but once the electricity was installed, he rarely milked a cow. Men did most of the buying and selling, apart from dealing with poultry and egg sales, the latter being viewed as the responsibility of women. My grandmother fed calves and milked cows, but she didn't bring cattle to the fair. This was viewed as a job for men and very few women attended the fairs and marts. First the cattle had to be walked to Carlow's Fair Green, a distance of twelve miles from our farm. A couple of times a year George and some neighbours would join forces and escort all their cattle together – one man walking behind, another guiding the cows in front and others stopping the animals ambling down the various gaps along the way.

Some buyers would come out along the road to meet the farmers, telling them trade was bad and offering them ridiculously low prices for their animals. Sometimes they criticised the quality of the cattle in an attempt to deflate the farmers' spirits so far that they would accept low offers. Despite these tricks, the fair was always a hive of activity, as cattle stood patiently while buyers and sellers haggled. Most buyers were sending the cattle to England to be fattened there and, once the deal was struck, it was the farmer's responsibility to walk the cattle to the train station and see that they were loaded onto the train to Dublin, from where they were shipped across the Irish Sea. Farmers received their money once the cattle were on the train. If a sale wasn't agreed, the farmer had to bring the cattle home again. That happened to George once: he and the buyer couldn't agree over a difference of ten shillings in a sale price of £50 to £60 per animal. He lost the sale and had to walk them home. Maybe he was calm and resigned, but it sounds a very disheartening trip to me.

Once the animals were safely on the train and the money in their pockets, the majority of farmers went to the pub for the evening – most of them knowing a wife, sister or workman was at home taking care of the yardwork. This was one of the highlights of their year, a time to celebrate their hard work with other farmers. As a neighbour once said to Dad, 'I'd be an alcoholic only I'd nivir afford it.'

After one fair, a neighbour was so inebriated that Dad's older brother Georgie took him to the hospital instead of bringing him home. George collected him the next morning and he blamed Georgie for his predicament, saying, 'George, ye always braught me home, you'd nivir have dun that on me.' He then had to go to the local pub for the 'haler': a few drinks to get him through the day.

My grandmother Lily married young and had nine children – she worked hard both inside and outside the house. She milked cows, fed calves, kept hens, reared turkeys, churned butter, cooked, washed, baked and whenever she did manage to sit down in the evening she was always knitting a jumper or darning socks. She wasn't in any way a fashionable woman;

she wore, like many working women of her generation, a housecoat cum wraparound apron to protect her clothes. These aprons were multi-purpose garments, serving also as oven gloves, transporters of eggs or kindling, and even as dusters if an impromptu visitor was spotted heading towards the front door. Lily did have a good coat and hat, but she would make sure these lasted her at least ten years. She enjoyed company and chat, but she didn't go out to find it, letting visitors call up to her. Once a month, George drove her to the Mothers' Union meeting in Castlecomer, and that was about the extent of her social life.

Lily also had one annual day out that she enjoyed: the scripture exam day was a big occasion for children and parents every June. For weeks, the schoolteacher concentrated on ensuring that her pupils knew Bible stories, verses and hymns in preparation for the exam; she was determined her pupils wouldn't be outdone by those in the neighbouring school. Pupils from both schools were examined together, which intensified the pressure, as the clergyman asked each pupil twelve questions. They were awarded a first prize if they got ten answers or more correct, second prize for nine and third for eight. Anyone scoring less than eight had to do without a prize. The prizes tended to be a choice between a Bible, a hymnbook or a prayer book, but parents were generous with monetary rewards. While parents had tea and chatted in the hall, pupils went to the sweetshops up the town.

Like most farm wives of the time, Lily had her allocated tasks for various days of the week. Monday was washing day, when the water was hauled to the kitchen and, before she got the wringer washer, had to be heated on the range. Tuesday was ironing day. She sent her homemade butter to town on a Thursday with George. Each family's butter had a distinctive taste depending on the amount of salt used and what the cows were eating – and so people would come into the shop to request butter from particular farmers, be it Sixsmiths or Bradleys or Dalys. Saturday was Lily's baking day, in readiness for the Sunday visitors.

Although women didn't seem to be the main decision-makers on farms, that wasn't necessarily the case. When I attended a historical agricultural conference recently, I was intrigued by one speaker's findings regarding the power of the farmer's wife. She had conducted research with farm advisors from the 1950s, a time when they were trying to get farmers to modernise: to install piped water, to use some 'modern practices' to improve the health of and to improve the quality of feed for livestock. A common tactic was to chat to the farmer's wife for ten minutes on her own. Once the advisor in question convinced her of the advantages changes would bring to the farm's profitability and herd health, he knew she would convince the farmer to adapt.

Yet, even nowadays, some dismiss the power of the farm wife at their peril. I've heard of women being dismissed or even insulted by salesmen while their husbands sign up to some scheme, or machinery or seeds. Next morning, though, it is the farm wife who phones the bank to cancel the direct debit!

Roles started to change somewhat from the mid-1970s. The marriage bar – a policy that limited a woman's right to continue employment after marriage – existed until 1973 for most jobs. There was also the broader societal expectation that a married woman's place should be in the home rather than in paid employment.

A year or two after getting married, Mum was helping her old employers out for a week in their jewellery shop while other staff were on holidays. A customer came in and said at the top of her voice, 'Can your husband not afford to keep you?' My mother realised that, whether they liked it or not, her not working outside the home had bestowed status on the farming couple. That private choice showed the outside world that their farm must be making money.

As time went on, a wife who had a career in teaching or nursing was viewed as a 'laying hen'. A teacher was able to help out on the farm during the long summer holidays and apparently her salary was the equivalent to having an extra twenty cows, so the income was there without the work of milking more cows.

Mum was a typical farm housewife, yet her role extended beyond cooking, cleaning and childcare, as she took care of the increasing amount of paperwork required to run a farm. She would usher salesmen and visitors to the farm into the kitchen and, while having a chat, would also offer a cup of tea and a freshly baked slice of cake or a scone. When I was young, Mum sewed summer dresses for me and my sister. If we were ever sick and had to stay at home from school, she was always there. If we needed lifts to see friends, she drove us.

I didn't see myself becoming a farmer when we first moved back to Ireland. Our son Will was a tiny baby and I felt I needed time to acclimatise to rural living. I'm a confident kind of person, but I wasn't convinced that I could be a full-time farmer, that I had the ability to be a good herdsperson, and I didn't know if I wanted to try to fit into a male-dominated occupation.

Time brings change. I wanted the best of both worlds, to be a mum and to run my own business. I think many women now, just like I did, try to do it all and then realise we can't do everything. Having children, we want to be there for them when they come home from school. We need an off-farm income so we try to maintain a career or set up a business, often working late into the night when the children are asleep. We try to help out on the farm, perhaps conscious that the in-laws and neighbours will be watching.

It took over a decade for me to decide that I wanted to farm full-time and even now I'm writing as well as farming. But like my forebears before us, our family is working as a team. Are our jobs on the farm decided by our gender? Some are. Others are decided by our talents, our preferences and our failings. It's really nice working alongside your best friend and neither Brian nor I would be able to do it without the other.

ADVENTURES IN SUGAR BEET

My grandfather George was a huge fan of growing sugar beet. It was marketed to farmers as a cash crop, as it was a product that delivered an income during winter months, which were a lean time of the year financially. It had other benefits, as farmers could use the waste product of beet tops to feed their livestock, and they could buy beet pulp from the factory, which was also a good food source for livestock. To encourage farmers to grow this crop, beet growers got extra sugar rations during the Second World War. This was seen as a huge advantage, so some farmers grew beet just to get more sugar.

Although the produce and income from beet was very

much seen as a win–win from the farmer's perspective, the crop wasn't at all popular with the teenagers and workmen who had to sow, thin and harvest it, as the work could be gruelling.

Very few farmers grew beet in Crettyard, even though the sugar factory was only twelve miles away on the other side of Carlow town. Allegedly it could be grown on any arable land, but it wasn't an easy crop to grow well. An average yield was fourteen tons to the acre. It was planted in April, and needed a lot of fertiliser, weeding, thinning and general attention during the summer. The harvest began in October and ran until the end of December – the coldest, wettest, stormiest months of the year. It was particularly resented because, previously, these were the months farmers enjoyed as rest months. The harvest was finished, the livestock were indoors and most work could be completed either in a shed or in the shelter of the yard, not out on a frozen and exposed field.

The growers were advised that the land had to be deep ploughed for a successful crop. For many farmers, this threw up stones that hadn't ever seen the light of day and all had to be picked and removed from the land.

When Dad was young, all the work was completed by hand. The youngsters kneeled on sacks along by each drill, weeding and thinning the beet during the summer months. As they got older, they used a hoe to knock out the weeds.

The Sixsmiths grew three acres of sugar beet, which doesn't sound a lot, yet it kept them busy for weeks. When harvesting in winter, they wore waterproof aprons to protect themselves from the weather. The harvesting was a slow process, as the beet had to be pulled by hand. They tugged two beets at a time from the frozen ground, one in each hand, then hit them against each other to knock off the worst of the clay. The beets were put into piles, with the roots in and leaves facing out. If it was going to be frosty, the pile was covered with beet tops, as frozen beet deteriorated quickly and was unfit for the manufacture of sugar.

One year, cattle from the neighbouring field broke into High Shores and ate the beet tops. This meant there were no leaves to tug when trying to remove the beets from the cold, hard ground. The men couldn't use a pitchfork or spade for fear of damaging the beets, so they had to dig with their fingers to manoeuvre the plants out 'by the shoulder'. Dad can remember kicking at them – both in frustration and to shift them out of the solid ground.

The farmers were usually given a week's notice of a date to have their load of beet ready for collection. Meeting the deadline was crucial, as if they missed it their crop wouldn't be collected until the very end of the season, and bad weather would affect the quality of the harvested beet left in piles. Getting the beets from the piles in the field into the trailer was a laborious process too. Each beet was picked up, held by the root and, with a clean swipe of the 'snaggers' (similar to a machete), the crown and leaves were removed, and the beet was thrown into the trailer. Once Georgie and Dad had finished loading the trailer, they had to unload the beets out into a large pile beside the road. As the trailer didn't tip up, the beets had to be thrown out again. The work wasn't over yet, as six ton of beet had to be forked into the lorry when it arrived. What a job! No wonder the beet crop wasn't popular with young people.

Dad stopped growing beet in the 1960s; he'd had enough

of the hardship, even though mechanisation had improved, but many farmers continued. Tractors and trailers lined the roads to the beet factory in Carlow every October, November and December, right up until January 2007, when the Carlow sugar factory closed after eighty years in operation. The closure was blamed on the EU sugar policy reform, which cut subsidies and quotas. As three other sugar factories in the country closed too, Irish sugar was no more.

A MOVE TO SPECIALISED FARMING

Older farmers often preferred the security of mixed farming, as it was an effective way to ensure money coming in from a different enterprise at various times of the year. With specialised farming, there was concern about putting all your eggs in one basket. The older generation were often resistant to change and, if they owned the farm, would frequently prevent a son from making changes. Expressions like, 'Why do ye want to rent more land/milk more cows? People'll be talking about ye,' were common. The old adage of 'pride comes before a fall' meant some were cautious about expansion.

All the same, there was a move from mixed to specialised farming among young farmers in the 1960s. Concentrating on one or two enterprises often required less labour and less machinery. Many specialised in enterprises that matched their interests and suited their land type. Garrendenny wasn't suited for growing crops, plus it was expensive to keep a variety of machinery for different tasks such as ploughing, tilling and harvesting corn. Dad's main interest was in dairy farming so cows became his focus. With the installation of electricity and increase in mechanisation, it was easier to milk more cows and gain more income. Programmes such as *Telefís Feirme* (*Farm Television*) were designed to inform and educate farmers on agricultural improvements. In an era when not many homes had television sets, the Department of Agriculture subsidised the rental of televisions so that members of agricultural organisations would come together to watch the programme. The presenter began by telling those who were watching in groups how to get the most from the programme: by arriving early, taking notes and discussing the main points once the programme had ended. Booklets were provided to aid the discussion afterwards. The first programme in 1965 discussed the types of housing best suited to farm animals in Ireland. Agricultural advisors became available to farmers with fewer than fifty acres under the 1968 Small Farm Incentive Bonus Scheme, who devised individual strategies to improve smaller farms.

With two hundred acres, the Sixsmiths weren't eligible for that scheme. Dad stopped producing barley and wheat, and the intensive nature of beet farming helped him decide to cease growing that crop too. The sheep had gone their merry way a few years previously. I can remember the sows being sold when I was about four years of age around 1973. I was holding Mum's hand watching as the last few sows waddled out from the pig houses into the trailer. As Dad was expanding the milking herd, the job of feeding the pigs after milking each evening became a chore that he hated. And, as whole milk was now taken by the creamery, it made financial sense to be paid by the creamery for the milk rather than feed it to the pigs.

Meanwhile, the number of cattle in the country, both beef and dairy, was increasing. In 1854 there were 1,117,000 cows, and that number was similar one hundred years later at 1,204,000. The size of the national herd started to increase from the mid-twentieth century, as rates of calf mortality decreased. The number of cows markedly increased during the 1960s, and had almost doubled by 1974, when it reached 2,208,000.[4] From 1974 until 2006, the only livestock on our farm were cows and their offspring.

Mixed farming is very rare now. We produce milk and beef from our dairy herd and many other farmers also have two enterprises, for example, suckler cows and sheep, beef and sheep, arable crops and sheep, and dairy and beef. To have a variety of enterprises as my father and grandfather once did is unusual. Poultry farming, whether producing chicken as meat or producing eggs, is popular in some areas of Ireland, particularly Co. Monaghan. Specialisation allows the farmer the time and the headspace to concentrate on one or two enterprises and do that as well as possible. As many farms are family run, and not many have staff, specialising improves the chances of there being quiet times of the year, which permit some time off and a holiday away from the farm. We go on holiday in January, sandwiched in between when the cows stop milking for their rest period and before they calve and start producing milk again.

3

THE FIELDS OF GARRENDENNY FARM

Most fields on all farms have names, primarily to aid communication. It's important everyone in the family and any workers know the names of the fields. There is less risk of going to the wrong field with tea or machinery parts for a repair. There's also less likelihood of communication breakdowns so that gates aren't left open when they shouldn't be, and livestock aren't brought to the wrong field for grazing, although of course mistakes happen. I'd be lying if I said that had never happened to me. But field names serve even more important functions than communication and convenience.

The name often says much about the field's size, shape, soil type and nearby landmarks. Many farms have a field called 'the Bog', the name reserved for the wettest field on the farm, or one where turf was harvested. We have two of them: 'The Middle Bog' and 'Byrne's Bog', the latter named after the family who lived beside it.

The Middle Bog has a nice family story connected with it.

Herbert Sixsmith, my great grand-uncle and the first Sixsmith to live in Garrendenny, was by all accounts a very matter-of-fact man. He liked to get things done without any fuss. He and a couple of helpers were pitching hay into haycocks early one afternoon when he stuck his pitchfork into the ground, rolled down his sleeves and reached for his jacket, saying he'd be back in an hour or so. He left the Middle Bog, walking towards Carlow, and returned within the hour. He didn't comment on where he'd been and the helpers didn't ask. Later that afternoon, Rebecca, his newlywed wife, arrived in a pony and trap with all her belongings ready to move into her new home at Garrendenny Castle. Indeed, he had walked to the church a mile away for a private wedding service and then left his bride to find her own way home. Romantic Ireland was certainly dead and gone!

THE CHAPEL FIELD

Most Irish farms are fragmented into at least two holdings, and many up to five or six. When expanding, the Irish don't tend to sell up and buy bigger farms. Their strong attachment to the land means they buy land as close by as possible. Herbert had inherited a hundred acres in Doonane, and lived with his parents. When he purchased the farm and castle at Garrendenny, two miles away, Doonane became his outfarm. The Chapel Field is one of the fields there. As you might expect with that name, there is a chapel located to one side. As recently as 1937, even though this field had a road running along either side of it, there was no vehicular access to the church. Both roads stopped one hundred and fifty yards from it.

Back then, most people walked from their homes in

neighbouring villages, up through 'the watery lane', which was really a shallow stream, over the stile of the Banks Field that exists to this day (although is seldom used), and crossed the road before walking through the Chapel Field to their place of worship.

One road, which still exists, travelled to the left of the field to go on towards Fairymount. The other, on the right side, went towards the village of Doonane. It was as if both ignored the chapel marooned between them. Why was that? It may have been that previous landlords or their agents weren't in favour of the chapel's existence. It was built at the top end of the field, with its rear to the road. Old maps show trees marked around the chapel; perhaps these trees were planted by a landlord to restrict use of the grounds as a burial place.

The absence of a road to the chapel may have been an attempt to get around the penal clause which stated that 'popish places of worship' should not be located in public spaces, so reducing its visibility to passers-by may have been deliberate. Of course, there might have been a practical reason. Perhaps the roads serving the local coal pits along the most direct routes were the priority.

Herbert made a deal with the council in 1937. He gave them some land beside the chapel, which they used to build a number of cottages with sizeable plots for growing vegetables. They also extended the road so it reached the church and created a larger graveyard. In return, they gave him the road running along the right side of the Chapel Field, which he returned to grass. This meant that his farm in Doonane was divided by just one road instead of two, which made it much easier when moving cattle from field to field.

The chapel is a nice backdrop to our black and white cattle grazing in the field – especially when we hear the bell tolling at midday and 6 p.m. We have to be mindful of church services on occasion, particularly when weddings or funerals are held. No bride would appreciate the scent of slurry being spread as the aromatic backdrop to her wedding.

THE BANKS AND THE BIG FIELD

No prizes for guessing the reason for the name of the Big Field. At twenty-seven acres, it is the largest on the farm. It was often used for tillage up to the mid-1960s but, with the exception of two years, has been in pasture for the last half-century.

The Banks Field was used for open cast mining, as the coal was very near to the surface. An English surveyor came to the area in the 1860s to report on the conditions of the coalfields and the quality of the land. His report stated the ground was poor and wet, not much good for farming and hence most farmers supplemented their income by carting coal. He recommended the building of more police barracks as the miners were 'much given to rioting'.[5] Doonane Barracks – a small police station with a holding cell – was located just inside the gate of the Banks Field.

My grandfather George tried to find coal in this field in the late 1940s. During the excavations, they were advised by neighbours it had already been mined twice. Only two blocks of coal were found. By the 1960s, it was a field of twenty-one acres of humps and hollows that had to be levelled to make it suitable for agricultural purposes. Some of the holes were ten feet deep, and filled with briars and furze. Before they could start filling in the holes, the scrub had to be pulled out.

A digger was hired and, eventually, the field was reasonably level. It's been in permanent pasture since then, grazed by calves and cattle.

THE LETTERBOX

Although the letterbox once positioned in the stone wall that runs the length of this field is long gone, this field on the home farm still bears its name. The letterbox once had an important function other than a receptacle for posted letters. A postman travelled the nine miles from Carlow to Crettyard post office with mail for the local dwellers. He kindly did some errands and favours along the way. For decades, first as a favour to Herbert and then to George, he collected the daily newspaper at Burke's shop two miles away and dropped it into the letterbox in the wall of this field. The letterboxes weren't locked then, so the children used to run down to collect the newspaper. The postman always got a generous Christmas box for his efforts. This practice continued until the newspaper was ordered on subscription.

The local postman who collected the mail from Crettyard post office and delivered it to locals was a burly man of about twenty stone, who rode an old black bicycle around the lanes and narrow roads of Crettyard and Garrendenny. Whenever one of the children spotted him making his way up the long lane, they ran to relieve him of his cargo. If he delivered letters to any of the houses on Garrendenny Lane (located along the top side of our land), he would then cycle down through the grassy fields to the castle.

THE LAWN AND TOP OF THE LAWN

Until the early 1980s, there was one field with an avenue

meandering its way from the Lord's Gate to the Sixsmiths' dwelling house and farmyard. The entrance gate was given this grand name from the time the Butlers lived at Garrendenny. The Sixsmiths simply referred to it as the 'road gate', perhaps not wanting to be accused of being pretentious. The name 'the Lawn' evokes images of extensive parkland with established trees and well-manicured grass. In reality it was more like a sea of tussocks, rushes and bundages. A bundage is a clump of briars, great for growing blackberries but not so good for growing grass. The only thing the Lawn did have to boast about was two fine ash trees, one either side of the avenue.

In the mid-1980s, the field was divided into two. The ash tree in the seven-acre section on the left, the one still called the Lawn today, was hit by lightning and fell. The other section was given the imaginative name of Top of the Lawn. It is about four acres and its own ash tree was one of the oldest in the country. Its girth measured an impressive twenty-two feet and professionals occasionally came to ensure it was still in a healthy state. Sadly, about six years ago it fell during a strong storm in August. The tree split into three parts, each one falling in a different direction. As the cows often used the tree for shelter against strong sunshine or rain, we counted our blessings they weren't grazing there that day. It felt like the end of an era; this huge, magnificent tree – the first thing people over so many decades saw as they came in through the stone pillars at the road gate – was no more. But we are practical people – and the silver lining was it provided excellent firewood! One day, as I was walking with the children to the school bus, one of the 'tree assessors' drove in. For a split second, judging by the look of horror on his face, he thought we had felled that ancient tree deliberately.

Dad had taught his young cousin Cecil how to ride a bike in that field. He would run along beside Cecil, holding onto the back of the saddle to steady him – there were no stabilisers back then. Cecil managed to cycle faster and faster and whether Dad, at fourteen, couldn't keep up or simply lost interest, he let go and was delighted to see Cecil's legs maintain their pedalling as he stayed upright on the bicycle. The field was flat at the top and, like most of our fields, had a steep slope down to the road. As Cecil went to turn the bike around to cycle back, somehow he started cycling down the hill instead. He stopped pedalling, but the brake-less bike was gaining speed and heading straight for an electricity pole. Cecil wasn't wearing a hat let alone a helmet. When he was only a few feet from the pole, still heading straight for it, the bike suddenly hit a bump and wobbled. It jolted to the right, far enough to escape hitting the pole, before falling to the side and flinging the fortunate Cecil off.

HIGH SHORES AND LOW SHORES

Most of our fields are named after families who either owned the field in the past or lived in a cottage on or beside it. Some moved away decades or even centuries before I was born, either moving abroad for better opportunities or having been evicted by landlords in the nineteenth century.

High Shores is one of our favourite fields. Brian likes it because it is our driest field. When conditions are proving difficult on our heavy soils, the cows can still graze High Shores without doing damage. I love it whatever the weather is doing. When the wind is blowing a gale and the grey sky is merging with the dark hues of the horizon, I can stand up there and feel exhilarated. The wind may be blowing my breath down my mouth and throat, but the fields stretch out beneath me, making me feel like a giant who could put her feet on each patchwork field and march all the way to the horizon. On calm bright days, the horizon is much further away, and the 'top of the world' feeling still thrills me. Kate, our daughter, experiences the same exhilaration when walking across that field, which makes me wonder whether it's a female thing – a case of like mother like daughter? A walk across hilly fields with fine views always results in us coming home in much better moods, relaxed and empowered all at once.

High Shores is now divided into two: the top half is flat and backs onto Garrendenny Lane; the bottom half slopes down, parallel with the wood I used to think was so huge when I was a child seeking adventures and trees to climb. There's history here too: there were two large hollows where gravel was dug out by hand in the 1930s, for building projects. Perhaps the gravel was used for the hayshed, built in 1932, and still used every year for storing straw. We filled in one of the hollows this year as it tended to become a pond during wet weather. Nice for wild ducks, but not so good for the grazing cows. We removed the topsoil and covered the hole with many loads of earth dug out when making room for a new shed in the farmyard. The topsoil was replaced and grass seeds sown. In one way we were removing history; in another, we were creating it by improving the field.

Herbert purchased High and Low Shores sixteen years after purchasing the original farm. They were owned by a small farmer, John Shore, who also worked as a carman. He lived nearby and he had right of way up along the avenue to the gateway at Low Shores. He rose early and set off with his horses and cart to collect coal from the mines and then deliver it. Except one day it came to Herbert's attention that these horses weren't being grazed on Low or High Shores at night, but were in fact being retrieved early from Herbert's fields. They were put into Low or High Shores in the afternoon, but at some stage during the late evening the gate was opened and they were being let out to graze Herbert's grass. Hoof marks were spotted in fields that Herbert knew his own horses hadn't been in. One night, he and his workman, knowing the carman's horses had been newly shod, caught both of them, led them to the stable and removed their shoes before releasing them. Funnily enough, the unwelcome grazing stopped.

Soon afterwards Herbert purchased both fields from Shore. High Shores is the field that holds more memories for me. We walked there to visit neighbours on winter evenings when the snow was four inches deep and the full moon meant there was no need for torches. Like ramblers of the past, we climbed over a gate to get out onto the lane and tramped along the rough ground in boots, muffled up with hats and scarves against the cold. After tea, whisky and chat in the neighbour's house, it was time to ramble home again. Once it would have been relatively busy for a rural country lane but, unlike times gone by, we didn't meet anyone on our way home.

There was also the windy day I was riding my pony there. Lucy didn't want to ride into the wind, but we'd gone a distance with the wind behind her, so she had to turn around. Lucy's stubbornness matched mine, but she had the advantage of strength. Whether she decided she would join me in the exhilaration of running into the wind or felt that the handiest way to get rid of me was to bolt, off she suddenly took. She reared up and I ended up on the ground. Dad was fencing nearby and got a shock when he saw Lucy bolting down the hill and no sign of me. He was convinced I was on the other side of her, my foot caught in the stirrup as I was dragged along. I then appeared over the brow of the hill, cross that Lucy had outsmarted me and determined not to let her get away with it. I got back on eventually, but we both knew that she had won the battle as we rode home with the wind behind us.

Low Shores has many springs and has been drained a few times. It has a steep sandy bank leading to a peaty hollow. The first water pump was placed there to bring to the yard and house. When we reseeded it a few years ago, a tree trunk buried in the peaty hollow emerged. It was perfectly preserved and just might become a mantel in my new kitchen.

LYNAM'S HILL

Lynam's Hill was home to Jimmy Lynam. He didn't own that field but owned three others nearby. However, his thatched stone cottage and shed were on the edge of the field, hence it got the name. Whatever it was called in previous centuries is now forgotten. The local dialect changed Lynam to Lynup, so it's known to us as Lynup's Hill.

Jimmy wasn't born or reared there. His mother died when he was young and his only memory of her was of being held by a woman sitting in a kitchen, talking to another woman, and he always wondered which one was his mother. He inherited the farm and cottage from an uncle, moving in in

1928. Like so many men of this era, he remained a bachelor, living alone except for the occasional visit from his brother, who worked abroad. Of medium height and strong build, he wasn't a man to use his own strength, preferring others to use theirs. He and other farmers along the lane helped each other with jobs like mowing and making hay. Paddy Wade owned a horse, so Jimmy borrowed it when he needed one.

Jimmy had six cows. As well as those cows having calves, he bought in calves and reared them. He milked the cows, but didn't bring milk to the creamery. A local deaf woman called for a pint of milk each day and apart from what he used himself, the rest was fed to the calves. He preferred to milk the cows with his hands wet, dipping his hands down into the milk to keep them wet – my guess is that the milk wasn't up to the creamery's hygiene standards! His income came from the sale of cattle, which were always finished well and a credit to him.

Jimmy's thatched stone cottage had one main room where he slept, ate and relaxed. A small storeroom held everything from buckets to boots. A calf house was attached to the other end. A shed nearby housed the six cows in winter. Jimmy didn't drink, but like other men along the lane he called upon neighbours to play cards and exchange stories. He read the daily newspaper and stood at local crossroads with other men, all similarly dressed in brown or black overcoats with hobnail boots. His trademark phrase was, 'What's the general opinion on what's going to happen?'

Jimmy had a loyal and well-trained collie dog, Floss, to get his daily paper for him. A small shop, just a room in a house, was located opposite the Church of Ireland church at the end of the lane, a mile from Jimmy's cottage. Floss padded along the lane daily, bringing back the newspaper and any other messages. Requests were written on a scrap of paper and tucked in under Floss's collar, to be read by the woman of the shop, placed in a bag and returned to Jimmy. When Jimmy died in the early 1970s, he left all the proceeds from the sale of his farm to local and church charities.

TAYLORS' FIELD

Taylors' Field lies between the Letterbox and the Bog. It's quite an unassuming field: an almost perfect rectangle, fairly flat, no large humps and bumps to make it interesting. It has the advantage of good road frontage. No signs remain of the stone cottage that was there just over a century ago, the stones used by my great-grandfather for some project or other. At one end is a small copse of trees where I used to play. The trees created a perfect leafy glade where I could pretend I was camping on my adventures inspired by the Famous Five.

Taylors' Field is named for the family who once lived there – a Joseph Taylor and his brothers. The field has some notoriety, as one of the Taylors was hanged as a convicted murderer in 1903. The murder didn't happen in this field, but one of the two persons found guilty was Joseph Taylor. The victim was John Daly, who lived in a five-acre field at Clonbrock, about three hundred yards from Taylors' Field, at the other side of the river. John Daly lived in a two-roomed cottage with his wife Mary and their two children, aged nine and eleven. They had a vegetable garden, two cows and a mare. He worked as a carter, selling breakage, which was small pieces of coal mixed with 'culm' (coal dust). Some time before 1902, when the murder happened, it was reported that his and Mary's marriage had collapsed and they were sleeping separately.

Meanwhile, Joseph Taylor was having an affair with Mary. Ten years younger than her, he had worked as a miner and a carter and was employed as a farm labourer. He drank heavily and was alleged to have hit Mary on at least one occasion.

John Daly was killed late one night and was found the next morning with wounds to his head. It seemed he was hit and stabbed with a pitchfork. Initially it was believed that Joseph Taylor was the murderer, but he claimed Mary herself had given him carbolic acid to murder her husband. The fact that her children gave conflicting evidence and that she didn't send for the police on discovering her husband's body meant her defence was weak. Her trial lasted a mere two days. The jury for Joseph Taylor took only fifty minutes to reach their decision and the jury for Mary took fifty-five minutes.

Mary Daly and Joseph Taylor were sentenced to death by hanging. He was hanged on 7 January 1903 in Kilkenny and she was hanged on 10 January 1903 in Tullamore. The case – known as the 'Clonbrock Murder' – received much media attention at the time, and was reported in local and national papers. Some reports argued that Mary Daly was unfairly treated by British law, as four other women (all British) were found guilty of murder around this time and had their sentences commuted to twenty years' imprisonment. It was argued that Mary received the death penalty because she was Irish and Roman Catholic. Her remains were buried three times: the first in the corner of the prison yard, then they were moved to a pauper's graveyard in 1937 when the

Tullamore gaol was sold, and finally they were brought back by her brothers to her home in Co. Laois.

BAKER'S HILL

Baker's Hill adjoins the top of the farmyard. It's a steep hilly field with a flat section at the top. It doesn't have the same 'top of the world' vibe as its neighbours, Lynup's Hill and High Shores, as it is more sheltered from the wind, but it has a peaceful atmosphere as I look across the valley to nearby Lynup's Hill, with its quarry and trees.

It was named after a tenant family. They were evicted during the Warren ownership between 1876 and 1904. The land was poorer then and was mostly given over to the growing of oats and potatoes. Like many other estate owners of the time, the Warrens set about consolidating the estate by clearing away uneconomic holdings and unprofitable tenants. Some evicted tenants were reinstated on new farms after the Land Acts of 1902 to 1903, others emigrated or stayed destitute. The Warrens evicted other families at this time too. A granite pillar marking what was once the entrance to the Baker cottage still stands in the ditch by the lane. Presumably there was once a second pillar there. Every time I see that roughly chiselled pillar, I ponder about what it bore witness to – the Baker family as they leaned against it watching out for people to pass by, neighbours calling in, donkeys or horses towing carts filled with coal going along the lane, barefoot children on their way to school, men rambling in the evenings to play cards and catch up on local news.

My great-grandfather, Joseph Sixsmith, died on Baker's Hill in 1959. He had a stroke as he was clearing away stone that remained from the derelict stone cottage. When he didn't return for his dinner, someone went looking for him. Unfortunately his time was up, but as a part-time farmer and builder, he died doing something he loved: working with stone, on a hillside with a view of the farmyard and surrounding fields. A doctor was called and said nothing could be done, that he would die within two days. He was right; Joseph didn't regain consciousness and died two days later.

My favourite memories of Baker's Hill are from December 2010. Heavy snow had fallen and we were snowed in for two weeks, only able to leave the farm by tractor. The milk lorry had struggled to get up and down the avenue, and as it was so difficult to get the milk collected we dried off the cows earlier than normal. The cows got an extra week's holiday; their lazy routines of eating, chewing the cud and sleeping weren't interrupted by the milking machine until they started calving in early February. Long stalactites of ice hung from the edges of shed roofs and we spread salt on the yard to melt the ice each day. The fields were completely white, with dark skeletal trees standing proud among the snow-dusted hedges. Snow creates more work, but it also brings time for fun. A tall snowman was built in the garden and we went sledging with the children down Baker's Hill. In the absence of proper sledges, we used the two halves of the children's plastic sandpit, the type that had a lid to keep out cats and other animals. We tied ropes to the handles, which made towing them up the hill fairly easy. I fitted into one with Kate, and Brian was in the other with Will. It was girls against the boys for the races down the steep hill. Then the children wanted to sledge on their own. We had our hearts in our mouths when we realised that our absence made the sledges go so much faster. Kate's sledge was flying towards a ditch with a barbed wire fence. Luckily it swerved to the left and came to a stop on the flat surface. They didn't get as big a push off the next time!

WADE'S AND BURKE'S

These two fields were purchased in the 1990s. They originally belonged to Jimmy Lynam. Unfortunately, the original names have been lost. Burke's is named after the previous owner and Wade's is named for the family who lived further down the lane until the late 1970s. The children often laugh about the time we were all picking wild mushrooms in Wade's. There was a particularly good harvest as the weather had been warm but moist, when along came a heavy downpour and we all got soaked. Soggy or not, the mushrooms made a delicious supper. Burke's provides lots of crab apples. One year, I was feeling particularly domesticated and made six batches of crab apple jelly. Even though the same recipe was followed, each batch tasted completely different. I wasn't so domesticated as to label them, so it was pot luck when selecting a new pot of jelly from the cupboard. There's plenty of wildlife too; one day, when driving towards the field, Brian spotted six hares in a long diagonal line, just their ears visible, before they jumped up and bounded off.

KERR'S FARM

In 2007, we purchased a farm of sixty-four acres. It adjoined our home farm; although separated by the lane, this wasn't a disadvantage, as it's seldom travelled by person, beast or vehicle now. When I was a child, the farm was owned by

Jack Bolger, a bachelor who had lived in the large farmhouse on his own. He had a sister and two brothers farming about three miles away and occasionally borrowed their tractor when he required one. When he sold the farm in 1981, electricity still hadn't been installed, even though 99 per cent of all rural dwellings in Ireland had electricity installed by 1975. The new owner, Hubert Kerr, lived three miles away and travelled to the farm daily to tend to his cattle and the land. Electricity was installed later in the 1980s as part of the Electricity Supply Board's commitment to connect all remaining rural dwellings for free.

The decision to buy Kerr's Farm wasn't an easy one. Could we afford it? Would the bank let us borrow that much? Given the strong Irish attachment to land and the reluctance to sell it, it was unlikely that any other land nearby would ever come up for sale. It would increase the number of fields available to the milking cows, so made economic sense from that point of view. It certainly wasn't prime agricultural land; were we crazy to be buying more 'shrubby wood and bog'?

There's been many a time when we've wondered if we were mad to buy it. Yet, in spite of the hefty repayments and the amount of drainage and reseeding required, a wonderful atmosphere of peace and a lovely old-world feel there makes up for it. It's at a higher altitude: maybe the thinner air affects our brains and blows all the financial concerns away. The views are wonderful and even better is the knowledge that you're completely alone. It's rare that we meet anyone along the lane and never up in the fields. The fields are of irregular shapes with tall hedging full of blackberries, furze, sloes and crab apple trees. Some farmers may prefer a greenfield site where paddocks are separated by wire fencing and there's little in the way of hedging or trees. Our farm has shelter on cold and wet days, shade in hot summers. In spring we can hear the cuckoo from across the wooded valley that extends beyond our fields. And if you listen very carefully, you'll hear the distant laughter of children from years ago above the birdsong. There are some things money can't buy.

What about the names of the fields up there? We weren't able to discover most of them unfortunately. The field in front of the house was known as the Hall Field. There's also the Quarry Field – and, yes, it has a quarry. It's an interesting field, as it has many soil types. When draining and reseeding, we discovered turf in one corner, a dry bank in another, and a rock breaker was required at the other end as the sandstone was so near the surface. We've had fun family picnics up there under two old ash trees, picked blackberries from the briars in the quarry, and when the children were as young as three and five, they were contributing by helping us pick stones.

We found out from a neighbour that the adjoining field was called Malantha. We had no idea what it meant, but detective work revealed that 'Mylanta' is a Gaelic expression meaning 'Oh, my God'. It is used so the speaker can't be accused of taking the Lord's name in vain. Perhaps the name came about as the field varies so much in its soil type. A quarter of an acre is a bog, which we don't even try to farm, and now it is a nature reserve, fenced off from the rest of the field. Two acres are quite peaty so are very good at retaining moisture. They would be described as heavy, susceptible to growing rushes but, having been drained, produce reasonably good grass. The middle acre of the field boasts a dry, sandy, very fertile bank. It grows grass of good quality with lots of clover. Years ago, the previous owners grew their potatoes on that acre and perhaps the wonderment of seeing such a dry fertile acre in the middle of rushes was what gave rise to the 'Mylanta' expression, and hence the name of the field. Maybe not, but until we hear a better story, that's the one we're sticking with.

We refer to the whole farm as Kerr's after the last owner, but have named two fields, Wilson's and Bolger's, after the two previous owners of the farm.

Many families and individuals lived in the Garrendenny townland and are long gone, but their memory lives on in the name of a field. I think it's a fitting, affectionate tribute to their lives here and it means they will never be forgotten. Some people have buildings or memorials named after them – isn't a field where animals graze and birds sing so much nicer?

4

STRAW TALES

Bringing home the straw was one of the highlights of our summer holidays, while the threshing day was the most exciting time of the year for Dad as a child. Straw, the stalk that is left over after the wheat, oats or barley has been harvested, is used for bedding. It gives animals a dry and comfortable surface to lie on. Although it is low in nutritional value, it is also used as a source of fibre in their diet, so it is very useful as far as by-products go.

Sixsmiths planted about twenty acres of corn at Garrendenny in the 1940s. It was cut about a week earlier than corn is cut nowadays, so the corn was still quite green when cut. This was to minimise the loss of ripe grains from the stalks during cutting and transporting.

In the 1940s, most farmers had moved on from cutting their crops with a scythe or sickle. They hired in a contractor with a binder to cut it. The machine also tied the corn into sheaves. A couple of people followed the binder, gathered the sheaves and put them into stooks. This meant the sheaves were arranged in a circle, leaning against each other so the corn could ripen a little bit more in the sunshine.

If rain threatened and the sheaves in stooks were dry, they were brought into the shed. If damp, they were put into stacks and left in the field to dry. If brought in when damp, they'd heat and rot, especially if there were grass or weeds in among them. A stack was a number of stooks put together in a large circle, with some sheaves capping them to protect them from the rain. My grandfather preferred using capped stooks to stacks. The stook was made as normal and two sheaves were put upside down on top so their heads of corn were downwards. It saved the job of making stacks and he believed it improved the drying, as there was more air around the sheaves.

The biggest excitement was reserved for the threshing day. Even with the improvements in mechanisation, the threshing needed lots of hands on deck. Twelve or fourteen neighbours came to help – this was known as a *meitheal*. No money changed hands; each farm sent one or two men, depending on the amount of labour they had available, the amount of help they would require on their farm in return and the size of the operation on that day. Pat and George went to neighbouring farms, replaced by Georgie and Joe in later years.

Initially the mill and pitcher – parts of the threshing machine – were pulled by the steam engine. Seeing it coming, puffing white clouds of steam into the air, created huge anticipation on farms. By the time Sixsmiths moved to Garrendenny in 1946, a tractor towed the threshing machine. The steep avenue to our yard provided the first challenge, as the tractors were small and the load was heavy. The contractor, John Bradley, had a Ford tractor that was up to the challenge, although everyone held their breath when it struggled on the top corner and breathed a sigh of relief when it chugged its way into the yard.

Men arrived on foot and on bicycles. There was a hierarchy to the jobs doled out, so sensitive choices were made. Two men, using grain forks, pitched sheaves up to two men cutting twines on the sheaves. John O'Neill, not so steady on his feet because of a limp but with a strong upper body, always took the job of cutting the twines. Some pitchers were enthusiastic at first, pitching three or four sheaves up at a time. The people cutting the twines got handy with their elbows and knocked the unwanted sheaves back down until the pitchers learned their lesson. Once cut, the sheaves passed to the man feeding them into the drum of the mill. It was a dangerous place to be, feeding the sheaves into the rotating blades, and this job was usually completed by the contractor hiring out the threshing machine. The blades snapped the grain heads from the straw and knocked the kernels off without crushing them. They then passed over a straw rack where most of the straw and chaff was removed.

The straw travelled up an elevator to be made into outdoor straw ricks or was ricked in a shed. The pipe smokers got this job, as it didn't matter if they stopped for a minute or two to light their pipes. The 'lowest' job was pulling the chaff out from under the machine to stop it from heaping up; this was done by a man who was unable to do any of the other jobs for whatever reason, or by a young teenager who needed to learn the ropes.

The last stage was where the clean kernels were removed. Two men took care of filling the sacks with grain – this was considered to be the most prestigious job. Neighbour Willie

Fennell was good at this task. Other men carried the sacks to another shed to be stored. Like most farmers, Sixsmiths sold the wheat and stored the barley and oats in the loft to be fed to livestock during the winter.

It was a busy day for the women of the house too; their job was to serve all the workers with two good meals for all their work – the first of these would be the traditional Irish dinner of potatoes, bacon and cabbage. The highlight for the children was bringing out the bottles of stout and lemonade halfway between meals. The children knew they could share a bottle of lemonade between two of them. Tea was cold meats and boiled eggs, followed by soda bread, spotted dick, tarts and cake.

Spotted dick, the white fruit bread, was always popular at teatime. Served warm with homemade butter and jam, everyone loved it. It was difficult to get white flour even though the war was over, so it was a real treat for many men at threshing time. One of Dad's uncles worked in a flour mill so, every so often, an eight-stone bag of white flour was delivered. One neighbour, Jack Lawlor, helped out at the threshing in return for George delivering his churn of milk to the creamery every day, and he loved this bread. One evening after a long day of threshing, he was in the pub and declared to all and sundry that, 'There ain't no point givin' white flour to anyone but that woman up in the castle.' A compliment indeed for my grandmother.

A number of contractors offered threshing services to farmers. Sixsmiths used Bob Boyle's outfit, although his machinery was older and subject to more breakdowns. One year, the men were nearly disappointed when it *didn't* break down: everyone was worn out as it was a very hot day and they were hoping for a belt to break so they would have an excuse for a rest. At dinner, Bob was jubilant. 'Wasn't tha' a grand morning's work?' he said, and all the neighbours could do was nod, weary and silent.

After a successful threshing day, bodies were tired, but it was a soothing and satisfactory tiredness, a feeling experienced after a day of work and company. As men went home by the light of the harvest moon, the farmer would count his blessings for having such good neighbours and good weather. The singing of the hymn 'All is safely gathered in, Ere the winter storms begin' would be joyful and loud the following Sunday.

SQUARE BALES

Dad stopped growing grain in the 1960s, so after that we bought straw from neighbouring farmers. By then, square bales were becoming popular. In reality, they were rectangular, about eighteen inches wide by forty-two inches long, but they have always been called 'square bales'.

I used to follow Dad around on Saturdays when he was bedding the calf houses. We had numerous small stone sheds in a terraced row that were used to house calves and pigs. He walked to the hay shed – it has always been called the hay shed even though it is used for storing straw – and lifted a bale using the pitchfork, balanced it over his shoulder, went to one of the little calf houses, opened the door, cut the twines and released all the straw, using the pitchfork to toss it around before shutting the door and doing it all over again for the next cow house. I trailed behind him, in a world of my own, walking up and down along the cobbles. I was perfectly happy doing that during rain, hail or sunshine.

When I was about eight, I was given the job of bedding the cubicles for the cows for their first night indoors that late autumn. A cubicle house is a raised concrete platform stretching along either side of a central passage. Metal bars divide the platform into individual spaces – or cubicles – for cows to lie down. Dad dropped in five square bales of straw, cut the twines and left me to it. I had a great time shaking the straw out, ensuring each cubicle had the same amount; I didn't want any cows to feel disadvantaged. I was very particular, ensuring the straw was spread evenly so each cow would have a similar amount under her front legs as her back legs. I wanted them to sleep well. It took me close to an hour to do the job that would have taken the men five minutes, but I'm sure the cows appreciated their first night of comfort indoors. Nowadays, the cows have rubber mats to lie on, which are fastened into place on top of the concrete cubicles.

EXPEDITIONS TO STRAW FIELDS

Buying straw from neighbours involved driving to their fields with tractors and trailers, spending a few hours lifting straw onto the trailers with pitchforks before trundling home again. For us as children, it was an exciting expedition. Our own trailer was quite small, so the men often extended it by lying two gates side by side along the base so they protruded a few feet over the end. It was then able to carry two hundred bales. We also borrowed a neighbour's trailer, much bigger than ours, so Tommy, our workman, drove one tractor and Dad drove the other.

We three children travelled on the Zetor tractor if there was a choice, as it was more comfortable. It had a wide cab with interior mudguards providing generously deep seats. My little brother sat on the passenger seat; my younger sister sat on the mudguard behind him, and I, being the eldest and apparently the most sensible, sat on the mudguard closest to the absent door. Back then, one of the tractor doors was always removed to save the time of opening it and to provide natural 'air conditioning'. It was considered 'soft' to have two doors on a tractor and the second was replaced only in deepest, coldest winter. We were always happy setting off with bottles of diluted orange squash and bags of crisps, knowing we'd be stopping for an ice cream on the way home too.

The brown and yellow fields looked so different to our green grassy ones, with the dark-golden spiky tops of the stubbly straw sticking up from the dun soil. The fields were dotted with neat piles of square bales, usually eight to a stack. The two at the bottom were placed on their side to limit any ground moisture soaking up into the bale. The next three layers were criss-crossed to the one below. Some farmers placed the bales in stooks in a long line – the term had evolved to mean bales, rather than sheaves, leaning against each other. When stored in this way, rain didn't penetrate the bales.

Tommy pitched the bales up to the trailer, where Dad put them into place. At first, Tommy threw the bales up with effortless ease with his pitchfork. As the load got higher, and the bales felt heavier, the throwing was replaced by a long stretch, and sometimes Dad had to lean over and lift the bale from him with his own pitchfork. Their lively banter at the start of the loading died off towards the end, as tiredness and a sense of 'let's get this finished' set in. I don't recall being bored while the men worked, although we probably were a bit of a nuisance at times. We entertained ourselves by having obstacle races over the bales. Sometimes I helped by lifting and pushing bales into place on the trailer or we rolled bales closer to Tommy.

Once we got home and the men were re-energised after a hearty dinner, it was time to unload the two trailers. It was Tommy's turn to be on the top of the load; he used the rope on the rear of the trailer to pull himself up. Then he used the pitchfork to throw the bales down as near as possible to where Dad was putting them into position.

Some farmers had elevators which worked like a conveyor belt. Bales were placed at one end and they travelled along until they either fell off the other end or were lifted into position. As we didn't have an elevator, sometimes extra help was drafted in. I recall one year when a neighbour was helping Dad and Tommy. It was nearing five o'clock and the trailer had to be unloaded if they were going to get a good run at the next day's work. Tommy wanted to get home to do his own farm work and Dad knew the cows, who loved routine, would soon be queuing up at the gate to be milked.

Tommy was pitching down the bales at speed to Mick, whose job it was to pitch them to Dad. Needing a break, Mick said, 'You two sure aren't good conversationalists.'

Dad retorted, 'You pick a topic, religion, politics, whatever you want, and we'll join in.' Somewhat understandably, given the suggested topics, Mick decided to stay quiet and keep pitching after all.

The bales were stored in the hay shed that was built in the 1930s: a tall building with a rounded roof which stood proud in the middle of the yard. The straw was stacked up so high that when we stood on the top row of bales we could nearly touch the roof. We loved the hay shed in the winter. Sometimes we found a litter of young kittens, which provided entertainment for weeks. We played at jumping from higher bales to lower ones before clambering up again. We never once thought of the risk of falling down in a gap between bales. They were packed tightly together and if a hole did develop, we knew to avoid it. It's not something to be encouraged nowadays; the large round bales carry more dangers, given the gaps between them. Their size and weight could kill if one fell on you.

KING OF THE CASTLE OR BOTTOM OF THE HEAP?

I was about ten years old the summer that Dad and I drew straw home from a neighbour's field for three days. The trailer seemed huge to me then, but when I look back it was tiny compared to the size of trailers carrying large bales now. My job was lifting and pushing the bales into place on the trailer as Dad pitched them up to me. My knees were scratched from the spiky sides of the straw bales and my hands were blistered from lifting them by their blue twines, but it was enjoyable work with the sun beating down and a soft breeze blowing. It seemed like the sun was always shining: the job promised hours of peace away from a younger brother and sister, and there was that sense of being the king of the castle from the vantage points on the trailer as the load of bales got higher and higher. Once each load was built, it was secured with two ropes and I clambered down the back, Dad pointing out toeholds while I held onto the ropes for good measure.

We'd trundle home and then it was Dad's turn to get onto the trailer; he'd pitch the bales across to the growing stack in the hay barn and it was my job to push and lift them into place.

The last load was only half full at four bales high so Dad decided not to bother securing it with ropes.

'Can I ride home on top?' I asked, not expecting his answer to be yes and so being surprised when he agreed. Dad climbed onto the tractor while I sat in the middle of the bales, prepared to enjoy the view and my new-found feelings of power and importance. The tractor eased the trailer out through the gateway and picked up speed.

I'd never been allowed to ride home on top of the bales before, and so I was on top of the world, sitting on the sweet-smelling straw as tractor and trailer weaved their way along the country road. Feeling superior as I looked down onto the occasional car, I wondered if the occupants wished they could be high up like I was. The breeze blew through my hair and I could see over the hedges into the fields of cows and sheep.

Was it better to lie outstretched or sit cross-legged, I wondered, as I changed position. Just then, the trailer wheel went into a pothole and the jolt shifted all the bales. They seemed to lift into the air and settle down again, but were they packed as tightly as before? I didn't think so. I felt that if the trailer were to bump again, the bales might leap into the air. Would they land back on the trailer or would they fly off and land on the ground? Should I hang onto a bale by its blue twines so that I travelled with it? Was I better off holding onto a bale on the right side, as it would land in the middle of the road, or a bale on the left, which would land in the ditch? Which was the best of a bad lot: being stung by thousands of nettles or being run over by a car? Or should I stick to the middle and hope that I'd end up on the boards of the trailer as bales tumbled off either side of me?

While I was trying to make this critical decision and imagining myself flying into the air, not at all confident in my ability to land on my feet, it seemed the tractor had accelerated again and was now hurtling along the road. I wriggled on my tummy up to the front of the trailer. By taking tight hold of baler twines and sticking my head out over the edge, I felt relatively secure.

'Daddy! Daddyyy!' I called. His hearing was never the best and now he appeared to have gone completely deaf, as he bounced along in the old Massey Ferguson, never once looking around to see if his eldest pride and joy was still on board. I gave up trying to call him and decided the middle of the trailer would be the safest. I wriggled back and gripped onto the blue twines as tightly as I could.

The tractor slowed as it approached our hilly avenue to the house and farm. I was relieved; at least I was out of the danger of being run over by cars if I fell off at this stage. Only four hundred yards to go, but now it felt as though the friction keeping the bales on the trailer was going to give out at any second, and they would slide off the end. I writhed my way up the trailer again until I was holding onto the twines of the front bales and lay in a star position, tummy down, and holding on for dear life. I made some excellent promises to God if only He would make sure I was still in one piece after that final stretch to the farmyard!

Eventually the tractor shuddered to a stop and I was still alive. As I told my dad about my angst-ridden journey, convinced I had narrowly escaped being flung into the ditch, I was disappointed to hear his matter-of-fact response that there was no way the bales would have moved. Still, it was the last time I pleaded to be allowed to ride home on the top of the trailer.

A STRAW BALE SLIDE

A year after that adventure with straw, we discovered I was allergic to it. As barley straw was the worst offender and wheaten the least, and knowing that drawing straw home was one of my favourite jobs during the summer, Dad decided to buy some wheaten straw from a brother-in-law. A condition of the purchase was that we could borrow his trailer to transport them home. At least double the size of our trailer, this was going to be a significant time-saver. Dad and I did all the loads together. Maybe we didn't stack them as high as two men would have done but we didn't lose a bale off any of the loads. I, however, decided to dice with death.

We had secured the ropes on the last load of the day and I was about to start my descent from the top of the bales, but Dad, seeing another farmer and my uncle come into the field, walked over to have a chat. (Some people say farmers are too busy to talk – don't believe it for a moment. Any opportunity for a chat about weather, yields, prices, animal health or anything else, and they grab it.)

I have never been a patient person and after a few minutes of being left to my own devices I tried to get down the back of the trailer unaided. After tentatively feeling around for a toehold and failing, I was nervous about going any further. It was too sheer, the ground was a long way down and I had visions of getting burn marks on my stomach if I lost my grip and slid down the whole way before landing in a crumpled heap on the ground. That would not be dignified, especially in front of strangers. But I didn't want to be seen as so pathetic as to need help to get down to the ground. How hard could it be?

So I had the bright idea of trying to climb down the front of the load. I walked along the bales and peered down. It looked a long way, but I knew the headboard on the front of the trailer extended halfway up the load. That would give me a secure footing once I got a toehold and, from there, I could jump to the ground. All I had to do was hold onto the twines of the top front bales and lower myself down until my toes found the headboard.

I was a little nervous but reassured myself this was no different from climbing down from the back. The men were still chatting away over near the gateway. I turned around so that I was facing the back of the trailer and got down on my hands and knees, sliding my hands in under two twines on the middle bale of the first row. I wriggled my legs back, my hands starting to burn.

I felt a rush of air and heard a thud. I opened my eyes to see three worried faces looking down at me.

I'd forgotten the top rows of bales jutted out slightly over the headboard so a toehold didn't exist. The bales were completely vertical and like a very slippery slide. I had got one thing right, but that was a fluke: there was enough clearance between the trailer and the tractor for me to fall to the ground, but it was sheer luck that I hadn't hit the iron drawbar with potentially dire consequences! Lesson learned.

The statistics relating to the number of people having farm accidents each year are startling, but I do think most farmers are more safety conscious now – maybe because we've learned from our own mistakes and used up a few of our nine lives. I'd never let my own children up on the top of a trailer load of bales!

Bringing in the straw always signalled the end of those long days of summer that had seemed never-ending. School was going to be starting again soon and our scratched knees, sunkissed faces and blistered hands would be a dim and distant memory soon enough.

PROGRESS

From sheaves and stooks to small square bales, and then to large round bales in the 1990s, progress was evident. Large square bales are now seen regularly too. The round bales are usually four by four foot, and although a person can roll them, they have to be lifted onto and off the trailer with a mechanical loader. Brian used to borrow a neighbour's bale trailer and would draw home three loads each day, usually during the last week in August, just before school started up again. When our son Will was three years old, he was adamant he wanted to travel home on the tractor for each and every load. We felt the ten-mile journey there and back over narrow roads was too far, especially as he'd have to wait and watch while it was being loaded. But I remembered that excitement of driving home with a load of straw, so I drove him to the straw field a number of times, arriving as Brian had almost finished loading. We'd have a small picnic in the field, a sandwich and a drink, and then Will would get into the passenger seat in the tractor, fastened in with the seat belt.

As he got older, he still loved the straw runs. He came in to play and rest while Brian was unloading the bales, but first he insisted on helping to take off the straps securing them in place. These had to be taken off in a particular order according to their colour and in reverse to the way they were put on. The journey to farms always seemed to be along narrow bumpy roads. Will loved the hills and bumps, roaring with laughter when a bump made them both jump in their seats. He renamed Ballinabranagh as Bumpy Branagh. A route via a rural shop always made it extra special, as there was a crucial stop for ice cream or some other treat as a reward for his help.

Now the workload has been reduced even further. We started buying straw from a different farmer a few years ago. We borrowed his trailer too, so he had a trailer loaded each time for Brian. When Brian arrived in the field he just had to unhitch the empty trailer and hitch up the full one, which saved him a lot of time. This farmer now delivers our straw, fifty bales at a time on his large trailer. He unloads them too, four bales high, in the hay barn. All we have to do is write the cheque at the end. It is progress in that there's less labour involved, but we have lost all that camaraderie that made the harvesting and drawing of straw so special.

STRAW TALES

There are a few superstitions associated with straw. If a wisp of straw trails after a hen, it signifies a forthcoming death. Straw is also said to get rid of warts. Rub the wart with straw, say a prayer and bury the straw. As it decays underground, the wart will disappear. In order to increase your chances of good luck for the forthcoming year, take a wisp of straw from the Christmas nativity scene at church and put it in your home.

The coming of the straw boys to a wedding celebration was an old custom, and said to bring good luck to the couple. The men wore tall straw hats, which were pulled down to cover their faces so they weren't recognised, and a thick straw belt around their waists. The captain of the straw boys wore a different coloured ribbon to distinguish him. He asked permission to enter and, once granted, he danced with the bride while the others danced with other ladies. He kept control, and if anyone misbehaved he had the authority to send them home. One night, Pat Patterson, our workman, borrowed my great grandfather's battered trilby hat (not having a straw hat) when visiting a wedding with other straw boys. It was important to maintain one's disguise, but he wasn't expecting my grandparents to be there. They recognised the hat and his identity was revealed.

A few years ago, two of our four hens disappeared. I presumed the fox had struck lucky and I kept the other two indoors, letting them out only for a couple of hours in the evening when we were in the yard. But then, while scanning cows at the cattle crush ten days later, we saw a hen stagger out from between the many round bales in the hay barn. She wobbled over to a large puddle and took a long drink. She must have wandered in there and got lost in what was effectively a dark and narrow maze. She would have found grain to eat, but nothing to drink. We never found the corpse of the other hen so can only speculate that her demise was due to the fox.

5

THE WONDERS OF ELECTRICITY

Tall and grey, four hundred yards from the main road and nestled in among a dense canopy of mature trees, Garrendenny Castle was often described as a 'poor man's castle'. Its original three-storey section was narrow. An arched back door with a carved granite surround, and a coat of arms above it, led into a small hallway with a flagstone floor. A door to the left led to the wooden spiral stairs in the stone tower. Straight ahead was the kitchen with its range cooker and a small breakfast room was to the left. Above, and accessed via the narrow wooden spiral staircase, was the dormitory. The room was twelve feet high with tall, wide, curtainless windows. Granite columns separated the glass panes and wooden shutters fastened back into the recesses during the day. The huge cast-iron fireplace was usually devoid of a fire. Dad's six sisters slept in this room.

Further on up the tower stairs were two attic bedrooms, low ceilinged and each with a small cast-iron fireplace. Dad and his brother Georgie slept in one room and the workman Pat Patterson was in the other.

The eighteenth century two-storey extension contained the sitting room, dining room, reception hall and toilet on the ground floor. Three bedrooms were on the first floor. The house had two staircases, one in the tower and one from the reception hall to the first floor. With eight children and four adults living there in 1949, anything that could help with the workload was going to be welcomed.

LET THERE BE LIGHT

The Rural Electrification Scheme began to install electricity in rural areas from 1946. Although Garrendenny is quite isolated, it was within three miles of one of the most densely populated rural areas in Ireland. The large population was owing to so many people working in the various local coalmines. Many farmers worked as carters, collecting coal at the pit mouths and delivering it by horse and cart for miles around.

In 1949 electricity became available in Moneenroe, three miles from Garrendenny, to serve the coalmines and the large local population. My grandfather really wanted to get electricity installed and campaigned for the Electricity Supply Board (ESB) to supply households in our area. However, Garrendenny Farm wasn't considered 'economical' enough; that is, the financial return wasn't enough for the cost of running poles across to us. A few farmers got it installed but we were too far away. And so George's campaigning was fruitless until the ESB decided to run electricity to a coalmine in Kilgorey, three fields across from Garrendenny. With a rent of £14 per annum to be paid by George, it was now worth ESB's while to install poles and electricity, and so it wasn't long before poles and wire intersected those three fields.

Rather than reading newspapers and darning socks by the light of the fire and a Tilley lamp, light bulbs now illuminated the kitchen and every room. As the light was switched on for the first time in the high-ceilinged kitchen and cobwebs from previously dark corners swung into view, the first reaction was to switch the light off again!

My grandfather, of course, wanted electricity for the yard. The fourteen cows that had been hand milked could now be milked with a bucket plant, two at a time, within the little cow houses. It was quicker and less labour intensive. One or two people could manage the cows easily and the herd expanded to twenty-two cows. However, there was a limit to the number of months the cows were milked by machine because the motor was needed elsewhere.

Electricity helped to save labour with another task: that of cutting up the turnips to feed the livestock. The problem was there was only the one motor. From November to March, the motor was taken off the milking machine and put on the turnip cutter while the couple of cows being milked through the winter months went back to being milked by hand. It seems silly now that another motor wasn't purchased, but that was what happened for years.

Gradually, all the sheds in the yard gained electric light. Neighbouring farmers learned how to become 'electricians' and extended electricity wires further in farmyards to more sheds in return for fifty cigarettes. There was another advantage to having electricity in the yard (or perhaps it was a disadvantage): work could finish later. Previously, cows had to be milked by 5 p.m. in the winter before complete darkness fell; they could now be milked later if the farmer was delayed.

The differences in the house were immense, and although they still didn't have piped water installed, my grandparents invested in a number of labour-saving devices within those first few years of getting electricity. All rooms, even the attic bedrooms, had electric light. An electric iron was purchased, which was much more convenient than heating two or three flat irons by the fire and using them in turn as they heated and cooled. An electric oven was purchased in 1950, which saved the headache of trying to regulate the fire and temperature in the range cooker.

A wringer washer was purchased the same year, even though water wasn't piped into the house as yet. Buckets of water were filled at the tap in the yard and carried the hundred yards to the kitchen. But it did save labour, as no longer did water need to be heated in large pans on top of the fire before scrubbing at tubfuls of clothes using a dolly stick and washboard. This new machine heated the water and washed the clothes. The clothes still had to be rinsed manually, but they didn't have to be wrung out with bare hands. They were fed through the wringer on top of the machine before being hung out to dry and ironed with the electric iron. Today we would view the wringer washer as labour intensive, but for the women of the time it marked a vast improvement.

A refrigerator was bought a few years later, the highlight being that a large block of ice cream could be purchased from the local shop and stored in the icebox waiting for eight teenagers to devour it. A television was installed in 1954, half a decade before Raidió Teilifís Éireann (RTÉ) started broadcasting. BBC channels were received via a transmitter.

The coalmine at Kilgorey was worked for less than a year, yet my grandfather was always grateful to it, as otherwise it would have been at least another decade before electricity arrived at Garrendenny. Some neighbours didn't get an electricity connection until the mid-1960s and one neighbouring farm didn't get it until the mid-1980s. Many weren't able to afford the connection. Much depended not just on the availability of an electricity supply, or the affordability, but also the family's attitude to modernisation. Some saw it as an unnecessary expense on the farm. Others were nervous it would cause a fire or the poles in the fields would be obstacles when ploughing and harvesting. And, to put it plainly, some farmers didn't see the need for electricity, as they had a wife and daughters to milk the cows.

Obviously, we are completely dependent on electricity now. It's not just for lighting and cooking in the house. The milking machine needs electricity, the milk tank needs electricity to keep the milk cool and the sheds need light for when we are checking on heavily pregnant cows. We do have a generator for those, thankfully seldom, times when the electricity goes.

One February night, the electricity went just ten minutes after the last row of cows had been milked. Inconvenient, but we were hugely lucky that it hadn't gone during the milking, especially as we'd been running late. I was feeding the last pen of calves, so all we had to do was check the pregnant cows. It's not easy to check them by phone torch, as the bright light can spook them. And as Sod's law would have it, there were two cows in the slatted shed with their

74

pins down – the ligaments either side of the tail bone had dropped, which suggests labour isn't too far away – so they had to be moved across the yard to the maternity pen. I was reminded that it was Valentine's Day when Brian commented on the romance of the dim lighting as we moved the cows. The romance of Ireland is alive and well when there are farmers around to point out a silver lining!

THE TRAVELLING SALESMAN

One evening in 1950, as it was getting dusky, my grandfather heard a rat-a-tat-tat from the front door. This in itself was unusual as most neighbours called to the back door. On the step stood a dapper little man with a black moustache, wearing a black suit and a hat, which he removed as he said hello. He had brought an Electrolux vacuum cleaner and wanted to demonstrate it.

He came with some credibility, as he had just sold one to a neighbour. Not only that, but he mentioned her by her first name. Sixsmiths had moved to Garrendenny only four years earlier, and with most people known by their surname, the Sixsmith family still didn't know the Christian names of some of the older neighbours. This guest of great consequence was ushered into the sitting room. If he had just sold a vacuum cleaner to Mrs Temperance Langrell, he wasn't going to be brought to the kitchen. Standards had to be upheld and there was a carpet and fire in the sitting room.

After making some polite conversation and removing his suit jacket to reveal a white shirt, black waistcoat and a gold pocket watch, he took centre stage in front of the fireplace. He asked for an assistant to help him demonstrate the power and skill of this sausage-shaped vacuum cleaner, this marvellous invention that would render the brooms redundant, make curtains and carpets beam with colour and ban cobwebs and dust if used regularly. One of Dad's sisters, Alla, then fifteen, finished school but not yet 'serving her time' in a shop away from home, was nominated to be his chief assistant. She was particularly enthusiastic, as it was her job to dust and sweep this three-storey dwelling with its two staircases.

Lily and George sat on the sofa, my great-grandfather Joseph on an armchair, Pat Patterson on a stool, while Dad and his other six brothers and sisters kneeled on the carpet in a semicircle. The salesman stroked the pale blue and silver vacuum cleaner almost reverently with his long, thin fingers – a contrast to the gnarled and calloused hands of the other adults in the room. He traced the word Electrolux stamped out in raised silver letters against a red block background. He asked for an old newspaper and shook out a double page, laying it carefully on the carpet as if it were a small picnic rug, unfurling a corner and straightening a crease. He unpacked the hose out of its bag. Snakelike, it curled around the hearthrug with the cleaning head resting against the hearth. Opening up one end of the vacuum cleaner, he let all the children peer into it in turn and then he shook it over the newspapers. Tiny fragments of dust fell out. 'You can see it is completely empty,' he explained, 'and now I'll show you just how much dust it will suck up.'

Alla ran to plug in the lead while the salesman slotted the hose into one end of the vacuum cleaner. After taking the cleaning head off, and with almost majestic poise, he flicked the switch. The cleaner revved up and he placed the nozzle near to the back of the hand of each child so they could feel the suction. He then showed the adults. Switching it off for a moment, he replaced the cleaning head, pressed the black button again and pushed it along the carpet. All the children leaned forward. Was there going to be a transformation? Would the whole carpet be sucked into that hose? Yes, the carpet's colours were brighter, the design was clearer, the pile in the carpet was rising up. He let his assistant take over and she vacuumed the area in front of the fireplace. When she had completed that, he told her to unplug the lead and he removed the hose from the canister. He walked over to the newspaper and opened the canister. A neat pyramid of grey dust, hair and carpet fibres lay on the black and white paper. All he needed to do was mention that it could be paid for with easy payments once a month, and he had a sale.

WHEN TAP WATER WAS SCARCE

Although electricity came to Garrendenny Castle in 1949, which was quite early considering its rural location, it didn't get piped water until much later. Washing the dishes was a lengthy process. Someone had to walk to the yard tap, fill two buckets with water and carry them back, preferably without slopping cold water into their boots. No longer did the water have to be heated in a heavy iron kettle on the fire, but it did have to be poured into the electric kettle and be boiled first. The hot water was then poured into the washing up bowl. Once the water became greasy, it had to be thrown out at the back door and the bowl refilled for the rest of the washing up. Once again, the greasy water was thrown out and the washing bowl rinsed.

By now the buckets and kettle were empty and my grandmother was probably longing for a cup of tea, so out she had to go for more water. Washday required twenty-two buckets of water.

Piped water was eventually installed in Garrendenny in 1964, more than fifteen years after the electricity. Why did it take so long? Maybe Lily was happy with her lot or didn't realise what a difference it could make to her workload. Perhaps she felt others might view her as lazy. My mother-in-law was told by her mother-in-law that she was too lazy to carry buckets when she insisted on getting piped water installed a year after getting married. They were more concerned about water conservation back then, it seems, as some argued water would be wasted if it readily flowed into the pipes and taps. Most neighbours hadn't got piped water either, so it wasn't a case of trying to keep up with the Joneses.

But it could have been for a variety of other reasons. Fewer than five per cent of farms (13,000 of 362,000) applied for and received the fifty per cent grant towards the cost of installing a water pump during the 1950s. By 1960, only twelve per cent of farmhouses had running water, yet by 1965 eighty per cent of rural homes had electricity. Was cost the main factor? The National Farmers' Association didn't want farmers getting piped water, as they believed it would increase the annual rate charge. They felt so strongly about it that they picketed a meeting held by the Irish Countrywomen's Association, who were trying to encourage farm households to install piped water.

It sounds like the ICA attempted to get their own back by creating the rumour – which I'm sure was true in some instances – that no woman would marry a farmer if there wasn't running water in the house. They argued that women were being asked to 'love, honour and carry water' at a time when technology was available to get rid of that endless, heavy drudgery.

Newspapers also tried to make farmers see sense by highlighting the financial benefits of running water. Numerous articles emphasised how piped water would affect farm profits by improving dairy hygiene and increasing milk yield. They stressed that farming was a team effort between husband and wife: that if women had various labour-saving devices such as piped water, they could add considerably to the farm income. The *Nenagh Guardian* calculated that if her source of water was one hundred yards from the house, the farm woman spent seventy-six cumulative days of the year just walking to and from it – time that could be spent much more productively![6]

In 1964, the year before my parents got married, piped water was finally installed in Garrendenny Castle. I'm sure Dad knew that Mum wouldn't be impressed if he asked her to carry buckets of water in and out the house when the technology was available to deliver it to the taps.

CROSS YOUR LEGS

Garrendenny didn't have a bathroom until 1964 either, though there was an indoor toilet, which was serviced by a gravity-fed supply from a spring on the hill. That was considered very modern in the 1940s – after all, people were accustomed to nipping behind a hedge.

One day in the late 1940s when Dad was about ten years old, he and his brother Georgie decided to play a prank. The adults in the family, along with Lily's three sisters and mother, had gone to a funeral and were expected back around 5 p.m. Women didn't go to funerals very often, but on this occasion they had all gone. The house was often busy afterwards, as relatives came back for tea and, of course, to analyse the ceremony. There was much to discuss. Was the eulogy accurate? Did anyone feel they had gone to the wrong funeral given the amount of praise heaped on the deceased? What about the choice of hymns: were they rousing and cheerful or too mournful? Was the singing good or poor? Who had a new coat and hat? Were the chief mourners sufficiently tearful? What about the size of the crowd? How many had to stand outside the church? Were they lucky with the weather or were they frozen in the chilly and windswept graveyard? What non-immediate family member dared to sit close to the front of the church? And, of course, who in the surrounding area might be the next to die?

Attending a funeral was a lengthy process. Between leaving home early to get a good seat, the actual service, the burial afterwards, followed by lining up to sympathise and have a chat with other mourners, the boys knew the ladies would all be needing to spend a penny when they got back home. But they had a plan: they got a broom handle and, sticking it in the narrow open window, they managed to push across the bolt on the inside of the toilet door.

When the ladies returned and took off their hat and coats, the kitchen was the first port of call. Water had been carried in and the kettle was on. A spotted dick and an apple tart were on the table waiting to be served onto side plates and devoured. One by one, the ladies stood up and walked down the hall to try the toilet door, returning each time to say that it was locked, someone was inside.

After some time had lapsed, the conversation was waning as bladders were threatening to burst. Lily knocked on the lavatory door and called to ask who was inside. There was no reply. She was joined by her sister Charlotte, who bent down to try and look through the large keyhole, the key for which was long lost, but could see nothing. What if someone had collapsed in there? They called all the children indoors and did a headcount – there were Lily's nine, Charlotte's one and Evelyn's two. All were present and correct. George came in to see what was going on. Charlotte was getting desperate. No one noticed that the boys' normally pale skin was flushed scarlet, making their almost white eyebrows stand out in stark relief. George put his shoulder to the door and pushed against it. It moved but not enough. He tried again and the bolt gave way. The boys scarpered off to finish their work in the field as a queue formed. Everyone assumed the bolt had stuck fast and they escaped a telling-off.

MODERN LIFE, MODERN WIFE?

My mother got a dishwasher in 1968 and, as you might imagine, at a time when some women were considered 'too lazy to carry buckets', she was the talk of the locality for being too lazy to wash dishes! I remember being on the school bus and another child telling me there was no point in having a dishwasher as you still had to dry the dishes. She was surprised when I told her that the steam dried them.

Mum's purchase of an automatic washing machine in the early 1970s was also frowned upon by her mother-in-law, as it was considered to be a waste of water and washing powder. One fill of water and powder in the twin tub washed all the clothes – from whites to good 'coloureds' to the dirty farming clothes.

I wonder if I would have been an early adopter of new

electrical gadgets or a bit of a Luddite. Last year my mum asked if I would like an electric soup maker as a Christmas gift. This soup maker was wonderful, she assured me, and for €130 you could chop your vegetables, pop them in and have pureed and delicious soup within half an hour.

But I like multi-tasking, and having a bulky object that only did one thing taking up space in a cupboard was incomprehensible to me. The conversation went like this:

'I don't need a soup maker; I have a large saucepan and a liquidiser.'

'But it's so handy and quick.'

'I don't have cupboard space for it.'

'What will I get you then?'

'Books.'

'But you already have so many books,' she kind of wailed. My mother seems to view my many bookshelves as dust catchers; to me they represent memories and stories and magic.

So, would I have been eager to embrace dishwashers, washing machines and electric cookers, or would I have been happy as long as I could read books by a Tilley lamp and the fire? I think I'm a hybrid. My dishwasher and washing machine are my best friends, yet sitting down in front of an open fire with a book is heavenly. I like to think that as a modern farming woman, I definitely have the best of both worlds!

6

THE ART OF MILKING

CHANGES THROUGH THE DECADES

Shorthorns were the dominant breed of cow at Garrendenny in the 1940s and 1950s – dark red, roan, white or a dappled red over creamy white, these were an attractive breed. However, news was arriving of the new British Friesians that were proving to be milkier than the Shorthorns. George's cousin Charles Sixsmith of Fairymount (three miles from Garrendenny), was the first to bring in British Friesians in this area. Although they yielded more milk than the Shorthorns and had a longer lactation, their butterfat wasn't as high. Charles didn't want to receive a lower price for his milk, so he had a trick up his sleeve. He tipped the churns of milk into the measuring tank in the creamery as usual, and when on his way to the office with his sample bottle of milk, he poured a little cream into it from another bottle in his coat pocket. The staff were a bit surprised when they read the results, as he had been heavy handed and tipped in too much, even for these new wonder cows. And so he was caught trying to pull a fast one. But when he died and the cows were sold, people came from all over to buy his Friesian stock.

Friesians were introduced to Garrendenny via artificial insemination in the mid 1950s, so the first cows were a cross between the Friesian sire and the Shorthorn dam. In the early 1950s, George was supplying about thirty-nine gallons a day to the local creamery. He had three churns – a fifteen-gallon churn which held the evening milk and two twelve-gallon churns for the morning milk. Every morning George made the trip to the creamery a mile away, first by horse and cart and then by tractor and trailer. He stopped at Lawlor's farm on the way and brought their churn of milk too. At the creamery, farmers queued in two rows for their turn to pour out the milk from their churns. They chatted and smoked, accepting whatever time it was going to take, although occasionally there were words if it was felt that someone from the opposite row managed to skip the queue.

As each farmer took his turn emptying the milk churns, he got help from the farmer in front or behind him to lift the churn up onto the platform and tilt it so the milk poured into the fifty-gallon measuring tank. Any farmer pouring milk into it twice, thereby supplying over fifty gallons a day, was considered to be a big supplier. These 'big farmers' were blamed for causing a glut in the market and keeping prices down. Compare that to today when three of our neighbouring farmers and ourselves are filling a lorry taking 28,000 litres (6,200 gallons) with two days supply of milk.

In the 1940s and 1950s, the milk went from the fifty-gallon container into a separator. The farmers took back the skimmed milk and fed it to their calves and pigs. A man with a horse and draycart transported the cream a distance of five miles from Crettyard to Castlecomer in twenty-gallon churns. Lifting a churn of twenty gallons wasn't considered a hardship, but must have been a considerable weight. The cream was made into butter in Castlecomer, branded with its own label and was considered to be 'very good butter' by locals.

On many farms, tending to cows was seen as women's work. Wives and daughters milked the cows and fed the calves while men worked in the fields. At Garrendenny, it was husband and wife, workman and sons who milked. My grandparents had very different milking styles. Lily, a tall strong woman, 'used to nearly put a hole in the bucket' such was the force of the squirt of milk hitting the bottom of the pail. My grandfather 'would nearly put the cow dry' his pace of milking was so slow. He used to smoke while milking, the cigarette dangling out of his mouth as his head leaned against the cow's flank.

As young boys, Dad and his brother Georgie helped initially by holding the cows' tails while they were being milked. This was to prevent the cow swiping the milker in the face with the end of a straggly tail, but also to ensure dirt wasn't swept into the bucket of milk. Dad's sisters didn't milk, which was unusual at the time. One day, one of Dad's sisters, Frances, decided she wanted to learn and was just about to sit down on the milking stool, having placed the bucket under the cow's udder. Suddenly, the bucket went up in the air, landing in the manger with a loud clatter. Jack Lawlor, a neighbour with a loud voice, had come into the cowshed while chatting and totally spooked the cow – not to mention spooking Frances, who left and never tackled the milking of a cow again.

The boys had fun with townie cousins when they came for holidays. One day, eight-year-old Cecil – now a retired clergyman and my godfather – peeked into the cowshed while some of the animals were waiting to be milked. One cow, a free milker who let her milk down easily, was leaking milk onto the floor as she waited her turn.

'That cow is milking herself,' said Cecil.

'Quick, put a bucket under her,' Dad said to him. Cecil picked up the enamel pail and placed it under the cow's udder, and within a split second there was a loud bang as her hoof hit the bucket and then another as the bucket ricocheted off the wall and the manger. She wasn't the quietest of cows and preferred to be milked by the same person at each milking. And so another potential milker was lost.

Once the farm had electricity installed in 1949 they lost no time in buying a bucket plant to milk the cows two at a time. The cows were slightly perturbed by this new contraption. 'You'd want to be hardy,' was Dad's comment on the training process. A couple of neighbours came to help for the first couple of milkings, and to see how it worked, and he, in his turn, helped neighbours when they got electricity and a bucket plant. They used to stand the cow by a wall, tethered by the head. The assistant kept her pushed against the wall and the person milking put his shoulder or head against her hip to try and keep her steady and stop her kicking. Some cows took to it quickly; others took a while to acclimatise.

A modern milking parlour was built in 1967 when numbers increased to almost forty cows. The cows stood in rows of four on either side of the 'pit', which is a long narrow channel with steps down to it where the farmer stood. The cows' hooves are at the same height as the farmer's thighs so the farmer doesn't have to bend to put the clusters on the cow's udder. Cows on one side were milked first and then the clusters were transferred to the cows on the other side. The first row of cows then filed out to the shed or field and were replaced by four more ready to be milked.

Dad also wanted to move on from the churns and get a milk bulk tank. With more milk being produced, the tank would cut down on the workload of heaving and washing heavy churns each day. Avonmore, the milk processor who bought our milk, was promising to introduce milk collections whereby they would collect from the farm, but they kept putting it off. Continued delays meant he had to buy a portable toughened plastic tank, which hitched behind the tractor and was trundled down to the creamery daily. It held the grand total of three hundred and fifty gallons. The milk was cooled by lowering a chiller down into it and removing it just before going to the creamery.

The concern about these 'big suppliers' still existed in the 1960s. A farmers' organisation petitioned the government to support the milk price of smaller producers and to penalise bigger ones. A multi-tiered milk price was introduced so a higher price was paid for the first fifty gallons. A farmer supplying over one hundred gallons got less for supply over that volume, and so it continued.

Dad was trying to expand at the time so wasn't a fan of this system. Hearing some men criticise the 'bigger farmers' one day when waiting in line, he retorted, 'If we were depending on the likes of you, we'd be importing butter.' Some farmers delayed expanding due to the multi-tiered pricing structure, and then found it more difficult to expand in 1973 when

Ireland joined the EEC (now the EU). Cow and calf prices increased and expansion became more expensive.

With the increase in mechanisation, milking became predominantly the men's role on the farm. Creameries were taking whole milk and the milk cheque was almost always made out to the man of the house. Although women were saved the job of making butter, they had now lost that income for themselves. However, women were seen as more patient and better at calf-rearing, so that job remained with them. I wasn't encouraged to milk cows. I don't think Dad was sexist; it was more that he didn't want me to be kicked by a heifer. He also disapproved of women milking cows while men were 'busy' at the mart, often not returning home until all the yard work was done. He felt women had enough work to do as it was.

There were ninety cows here when we took over the farm in 2003, and they were milked in a ten-unit herringbone parlour built in 1992. We kept cow numbers much the same for twelve years, as the amount of milk we could supply was limited by the milk quota imposed by the European Union. We concentrated on improving the composition of the milk through improved breeding and grass management, as a higher price is paid for better protein and butterfat content. We used milk recording to identify our best cows, we purchased A.I. straws of the best bulls available and we used genomics to identify the best replacement heifers to bring into the herd. Science now plays a huge part in herd development and improvement, and we've been able to double output. Since milk quotas ended a couple of years ago, most dairy farmers have expanded their milk production to some extent. We have increased cow numbers to one hundred and twenty-five, with one hundred and forty our maximum for the future. Many farmers, previously sheep, suckler or tillage, are turning to dairy. Those on large farms – more than five hundred acres would be considered very large in Ireland – are milking in excess of four hundred cows. Are there any complaints about these suppliers causing a glut in the market? Not as yet.

Expansion requires more infrastructure. Cow health and welfare is a number one priority for us. We built a new shed to house forty-eight cows a few years ago; a new calf shed for one hundred calves has just been completed and a renovation of old cow housing is also planned. The poor hardworking farmers could also do with a bigger milking parlour, so that is currently on the wish list.

WHAT OTHER PEOPLE THINK OF COWS AND FARMERS

Visitors to Ireland, especially if they have children, seem to love seeing livestock on the road. I've heard some say that one of the highlights of their children's holiday was to watch cows saunter along the road from one field to another. If the cows are crossing or walking along the road regularly, they display a very relaxed confidence and don't take any notice of the cars. They certainly won't speed up or move aside on the driver's account. For visitors, though, it's not a nuisance at all. They can take a photo and post it to one of their social media channels with the caption, 'What traffic jams look like in Ireland!' It could be said that farmers are doing the tourism industry a huge favour.

We used to walk yearling cattle from the home farm to the outfarm in Doonane every summer, but they weren't accustomed to being on the road so we had to plan it like a military operation in case they got away on us. All garden gates along the roads were shut and occupants asked to leave them closed. Mum drove in front of the cattle, the fastest runners and cyclists among the helpers got the job of stopping gaps along the way and then overtaking the line of cattle again to stop the next gap. Back then, drivers knew what to do in the presence of livestock. They took their time, stayed back, didn't rev their engines or glare at the farmers. Occasionally, they even jumped out of their car and offered to stand in a gap. What with the roads getting so much busier, people more impatient and fewer hands on deck, we now transport the yearlings in our cattle trailer.

In the 1980s, and probably before that too, neighbours half a mile along the road had a house cow. She lived in their half acre of land behind the house at night, but by day she travelled along the grassy ditches of the main road. She walked as far as our gateway and then calmly turned around and headed back. Everyone knew to slow down as they approached the corner, just in case she was standing out on the road. A quiet cow, she lived to a grand old age, providing milk every morning and evening, keeping the grass short along by the hedge and saving the council men some work. Sadly, having a cow out on the road unsupervised wouldn't be possible now, as the volume and speed of traffic has increased so much.

There's often debate about whether calves are removed from their mothers too soon after birth. A dairy cow provides too much milk for one calf, so she goes back into the milking herd and her calf is housed with others in a calf shed. It's like a fostering system, with the farmer as the foster mum. Scientific research recommends that calves are removed immediately after birth to prevent the calf getting an infection from the maternity unit, as it's impossible to keep the area sterile and the calf has no immunity when born. It's also recommended that the calf is fed at least three litres of colostrum within two hours of birth to ensure it absorbs the antibodies present in its mother's first milk. The problem with letting a calf suckle is that we can't know how much it has drunk. One litre wouldn't be enough to prevent the calf getting sick in the near future.

We usually leave the calf with its mother for a few hours. We keep the maternity unit as hygienic as possible, cleaning it out regularly and bedding it liberally with straw. I feed the calf by bottle, often while the mother is licking it. I have a chat with the mother as the bottle is emptying, complimenting her bonny calf and telling her how well I'm feeding it while she licks it dry. One cow had triplets this year. Triplet births are very rare and this was our second ever set of triplets on this farm. All three were hungry almost immediately – luckily, we had over ten litres of surplus colostrum left over from three cows which had calved that morning. I warmed up the milk and bottle fed them before leaving their dam (mother) in peace to continue licking and fussing over them. When I went to remove them a few hours later, each one was fast asleep in a different corner of the calving pen and the cow was resting in the middle. She didn't turn a hair as I removed them; she didn't even move, but looked at me as if to say, 'Thanks, love. They are gorgeous, but goodness, they're a lot of work.'

How does a cow react if her calf is stillborn? Thankfully, it is rare. If it was a difficult birth and the calf isn't displaying any signs of life, she might ignore it. A first-time mother may do the same. An experienced cow will know to expect signs of life and, if there aren't any, this can be heart-breaking to watch. Two years ago, I was with a cow that gave birth to a stillborn calf. She licked her calf clean and kept nudging it with her nose, as if trying to get the heart going and get it to stand up. We left the calf with her overnight in the hope she would realise, and to give her space to mourn. When we went out the next morning, the calf was at the edge of the pen and she was lying down at the other side. It seemed she had accepted the death, or at least understood what had happened. Thankfully, improvements in veterinary medicine and animal husbandry mean that calf mortality has declined significantly in recent decades.

THERE'S SOMETHING ABOUT COWS

Why do farmers farm? Is it because they inherited a farm? Is it the money? Is it because they want to live in the countryside? What makes dairy farmers want to milk cows rather than keep sheep or suckler cows or chickens?

For us, it's not all about milk, although producing a food that is a rich source of nutrients, and of excellent quality is something to be proud of. It's about the cows. Milking is Brian's favourite job. My favourite is bringing them in to be milked and feeding the calves. It's about seeing them thrive and flourish, checking they are healthy, knowing they are in good condition, taking pleasure in seeing their contentment as they chew the cud and stroll into the milking parlour. Our herd is now pedigree and we can trace family trees of cows back for decades. Do we have favourites in the herd? We often wish we could keep them all, but I have to admit that a cow with a good temperament who gives more milk than her comrades will definitely become a firm favourite.

Delilah is our highest-producing cow, giving over nine thousand litres per year. She always goes in calf first time too, which is significant as fertility can be an issue with some high-yielding cows. She eats a lot: she's not tall, but has a capacious belly to fill. All her daughters have greedy appetites too, showing that tendency from the first feed of milk, but despite the improvements in genetics and using A.I. bull semen, none of Delilah's daughters have been as fertile or produced as much milk as her.

One of Delilah's youngest daughters has just come into the milking herd. Delilah Beag (*beag* means small in Gaelic) is already displaying a greedy and curious nature as she continually tries to get back into the milking parlour to scavenge for any spilt ration. Her mostly black quiff has white hairs in the centre that are always tousled, giving her a 'I just got out of bed' look. She makes me laugh every time she pops her head around the corner. I'm really looking forward to seeing how she performs. It's that interest in seeing how daughters and granddaughters perform that really drives our love for dairying and our regard for cows.

7

TILL THE COWS COME HOME

Bringing in the cows to be milked is one of my favourite farm jobs. The cows are usually compliant and obedient. They know the routine. At the beginning of the season, the younger ones who might be uncertain about what to do follow the experienced ladies. As the year goes on and their udders lose that very full, post-calving, 'I need to be milked soon, please' feeling, they become even more relaxed and sanguine about heading in to be milked. They amble along, taking their time, walking in crocodiles of twos along the lane or cow track, just as their predecessors did for years. Rushing them would cause stress and risk lameness, so I stroll behind them, using the time to take an occasional photo, savour the peace and quiet, and smell the honeysuckle. Lou the dog paces to and fro behind them, ensuring they keep moving but not rushing them either. She listens to me if I chat to her, but doesn't leave her post for a pat or rub down. Getting the cows home to the milking parlour is important to her; Lou sees it as her most significant job in the day.

LEARNING FROM COWS

When I was eight years old, I discovered cows are much wiser than I'd ever imagined. They knew a lot more about life than I did, and have a much better sense of direction. Dad and I were bringing in the cows to be milked from the far side of Lynup's Hill. They were supposed to follow the most direct path back to the parlour but they decided to walk to the left, which brought them back up to the top of the hill. As Dad exclaimed in annoyance and set off to try and head them off to stop them going the long away around the quarry, he called to me to go back to the yard.

'But I don't know the way,' I wailed.

'Just follow the cow, she's behind you,' he shouted back.

As I turned around, I saw a cow, her udder almost reaching to the ground, with a slightly overgrown back left hoof, ambling on ahead of me. She didn't look to see where the others had gone. We strolled along the path between the wood and the mini quarry, she ignoring the badger setts to our left and the rustling of the leaves over our heads, focused on where she was going. I didn't know this then but later heard from Dad that she had been a matriarch in the herd, one of the leaders that the others followed. As she aged, she lost some of her influence but still paddled her own canoe, still followed her own path, still knew which route was the most direct one. As I walked along behind her, I marvelled at her calmness, her knowledge, her placidity, her maturity, her common sense and her sense of direction. As we emerged from under the canopy of trees ahead of the other cows in spite of our slower pace, I knew then that I would always learn much from cows.

When I was nine I graduated to being considered old

enough to bring the cows in on my own. I set off with our collie, Shep, who sometimes obeyed me and sometimes decided to disappear. As I got to the field gate, I shouted 'Aye' a few times and three or four cows raised their heads and took a few steps. The others sometimes took the hint and followed, but often they needed the persuasion of me walking up to them to keep them moving. In the summer, midges and flies flew around me and over the heads of the cows, filling my ears and eyes and nose with an irritating buzzing. While the cows swished their long tails from side to side, I resorted to waving a leafy branch around my head in an attempt to keep the pesky insects at bay. The worst were the horseflies, whose bites and blood sucking left itchy bumps. But all the same, bringing in the cows was a time to daydream, to admire the landscape and the clouds, to feel that my help was useful and an important contribution to the family farm.

What is now four paddocks – the Lawn, the Top of the Lawn, the Letterbox and the Top of the Letterbox – was once one big marshy field. The summer of my tenth year was a wet one, and the route to the milking parlour got increasingly muddy. As we got closer to the yard, the grass was limited to a few slippery narrow ridges of tussocks. I tried to work out which way would be the driest and opted for the right side. Three steps in and my wellies were stuck. I tried lifting my feet but the mud had settled on top of my rubber-clad foot and the mud underneath held fast with glue-like suction. All I succeeded in doing was removing my foot from the welly, and I was hopping around trying to keep my sock out of the mud when Dad arrived.

'You're walking through the deepest part,' he said,

somewhat unnecessarily, as he came over to pull at my welly, me holding on to him for dear life to try and stop my stockinged foot getting wet and dirty. Working out which is the shallowest or driest part of a wet area of field is a skill that took me a long time to master.

Bringing in the cows is my daughter Kate's favourite job now too. She listens to music, takes photographs of the cloud formations and chats away to her favourite cow. Number 1885 is always the last cow and is quite happy to get a head rub along the way.

FALLING IN LOVE ... WITH A COW

I fell in love with a cow for the first time when I was nine. She got my attention for a number of reasons. She was mostly white with red splotches whereas the majority were black and white. She always spotted me on my first 'Aye' and was the one to lead the others out of the field. She was usually the first cow in the first row in the milking parlour; indeed, I was disappointed for her if she was second or third. Her large eyes were kind and she seemed motherly and wise. I always scooped up the dairy nuts for the first two rows of cows and often gave her a few extra ones. I gave her the very creative name of 'the Leader'. I presumed it was her intelligence that made her decide to be first, that she was the chief among the cows, the wise one who taught the others. In reality it was probably greed for the sweet nuts she knew she was going to get in the parlour.

She was always the first cow out to grass too. She never hesitated when being sent to a new field; she sniffed the air, had a look to see what wires were up and then knew exactly where she needed to go. Not all cows are as astute.

Sometimes if the first half of the herd has already gone to the field, and more cows come out from being milked, they look around for about five minutes wondering where to go. They aren't leaders; they are followers and are obviously flummoxed for a few minutes. As a person with a terrible sense of direction, I sympathise completely and know that if I am ever reincarnated as a cow, I'll probably be in the last row to be milked.

After delivering a healthy heifer calf the following spring, the Leader went down with milk fever, which can affect high-yielding cows shortly after calving. The recommended treatment is to administer calcium into the vein but if that's not done quickly enough and the cow lies down, it can be difficult to help them to recover. She then developed gangrene mastitis. We'd never seen a cow with that before. Various methods were used to try and get the Leader on her feet. A sling was fashioned and the men managed to get it under her. As it was early April and reasonably good weather, she was lifted into the air using the digger and brought out to a sheltered spot at the base of Baker's Hill. We hoped being out at grass would give her more grip if she tried to stand up but it was to no avail.

But I never thought she would die. I was accustomed to stories ending in happily ever after. Even *Black Beauty* and *Lassie* had happy endings. I knew that animals and humans died, but I was still young enough to think that it only happened to ones I didn't know. Surely it wasn't going to happen to those I knew and loved?

When I came home from school the next day, Mum was away and the babysitter was there looking after my younger brother and sister. Somewhat unusually for that time of day,

Dad came into the kitchen. Even though it was out of the ordinary, I didn't think anything was wrong.

'How's the Leader?' I asked, expectant of good news.

To hear she had died was a crushing blow. Sensibly, Dad had phoned the knackery and ensured her body was collected before I came home from school. The babysitter told me never to cry over an animal, which struck me as a bizarre thing to say. It seemed wrong that such a special cow had passed before her time.

I named her daughter Polly – not overly creative this time either: she was a polled calf so, due to selective breeding, she didn't have horn buds to be removed. When she came into the milking herd two years later, I was eager to see if she would display the same leadership characteristics as her mother. I was disappointed to see that she didn't. She was always in the last quarter of the herd on the way in, very much a follower rather than a leader.

Despite Polly's lack of resemblance to her dam, some characteristics are innate and are passed down from generation to generation. We've noticed some mothers and daughters display the same behaviour even if they have never been together in the herd. We have a mother and daughter who both display a belief in the mantra, 'The grass is always greener on the other side.' They walk along by the electric fence and get down on their front knees to eat the grass, even if the grass they are trampling into the ground on their side of the fence is just as lush and green.

During calving season, when Brian and I are chatting while having our second breakfast, we'll be discussing calves. I'll say something like, 'That white calf is so greedy,' 'That little calf is very quiet, it's just as well she is in a small group,' or,

'That black calf born yesterday is a headcase.'

Brian will reply, 'Her mother and grandmother were the very same,' and he'll tell me a story to demonstrate the personality trait. Sometimes he might lament selling the grandmother or great-grandmother and end with, 'But sure, I couldn't keep them all.'

We do have more 'leaders' in the herd now. Rua, a red cow with a white star on her forehead, is always one of the first in to be milked and out to the field. Betty, a first calver, a small and compact cow, is also showing definite signs of wanting to be first. That's unusual for a first calver. She doesn't bully her way to the front but, even if during the winter she is in a group housed in the new shed, which means they are last into the collecting yard, she still worms her way up through the other cows and is in the first row for milking.

DEATH COMES TO GARRENDENNY

The expression 'where there's livestock, there's deadstock', while true, isn't an easy one to hear. Losing stock happens less frequently nowadays, thank goodness. We have more vaccines and treatments available to us and veterinary surgeons have more knowledge and improved resources. Years ago, when stock numbers were smaller, the loss of an animal was quite a financial hit. Losing a cow at any time can be upsetting, but to lose one from a small herd must have really hurt. It's worse when you lose an animal over something that might have been prevented.

In the 1950s, cows were fed turnips, hay and beet tops in the winter. Some farmers let their cows eat the turnips and beet tops in the fields but our land was too wet and heavy. However, my grandfather let them out one year as the weather had been very dry. Unfortunately, bovines can eat themselves to death unwittingly. The cows ate too many of the fresh beet tops, which were high in sugar, and this led to excessive fermentation in the stomach. One cow developed bloat, got scour and died. Another time, a neighbour didn't notice a newly calved cow had mastitis. He fed the colostrum to its calf, which died after drinking the infected milk. The mastitis wasn't caught in time and the cow died too, so it was a double blow.

The financial loss is one thing. It costs up to €200 to have a cow collected by the knackery and, of course, there's the replacement cost of the animal. But it's never nice to see an animal get so ill that it either has to be put down or it dies. We lost a lovely young cow last year, only in her third lactation. She was milking well but started losing condition. She was put on once-a-day milking in an attempt to help her recover and we got a second opinion from the veterinary practice as the treatment wasn't working. They concluded she had a tumour. She was still bright-eyed but seemed to be getting shaky on her feet as if her balance was going, so we housed her beside the milking parlour and continued to milk her once a day. She seemed to want to go out after the other cows, as she'd look after them longingly.

We were considering putting her in a nearby paddock, as the weather was good and she'd be more comfortable. But then she deteriorated. Although she was still eating, her appetite had diminished, and she lost interest in the other cows and seemed shakier on her feet. We thought she was on the way out, so we contacted the knackery to come the next day to put her to sleep. But the next morning, she'd rallied; she was standing and looking for food again, so we cancelled the knackery. It was unlikely she would recover, but as she wasn't in pain, we wanted to give her a chance. Yes, we were hoping for a minor miracle.

'She never shat on me in the parlour,' Brian lamented as he looked in at her. This was his way of saying she was indeed a special cow and he had a soft spot for her.

Two days later, she couldn't get up at all and wasn't eating. We knew she was dying and there was no point prolonging it if she wasn't going to be comfortable. We rang the knackery again and they said they'd arrive the next day. The next morning, she was lying quietly when I went in to give her a bucket of water. She started to drink and suddenly her head slumped down in the bucket. My first reaction was to think she had collapsed and was drowning in the few inches of water. I pulled up her head to lift it out of the bucket. I then realised she had died, probably from a heart attack, and I knew I'd better get out of the way in case her legs inadvertently kicked out and hit me. I jumped up onto the stone trough and burst into tears with the shock.

Although we were saddened to see her die when she should have been out in the field with the sunshine on her back and coming into the parlour every morning and evening, the silver lining was she passed away peacefully. There's nearly always a silver lining, even though sometimes we really have to search hard for it.

Daisy was another cow we had a soft spot for. She had twin bulls the first time she calved and went in calf again relatively easily. Sometimes it can take them extra time to become pregnant again after having twins. She was a kind cow, but totally clueless and rather clumsy. If a gate was open, she'd always go to the wrong side. She'd stop to examine something on the way out of the parlour and hold up other cows behind her. Sometimes she'd come back into the parlour to see if she could find any spilled meal on the ground and be a complete nuisance. Life in the slow lane was an adventure for her.

One dusky summer's evening, Brian was walking out to shut the cows into their field, expecting all of them to be grazing contentedly. Daisy was standing on the cow track, breathing heavily. He rang the vet and was telling him about her symptoms, walking her back to the yard slowly, when she lay down. Within seconds, she let out a loud bellow and keeled over. She was only five years of age and she was dead. The vet reckoned it must have been a heart attack.

The silver lining was that Brian was there when it happened so we knew the cause of death. He didn't have to experience a huge shock the next morning and worry if he had missed any warning signs during the previous milking. Thinking back, she had given a little less milk but not enough to make him investigate. Unfortunately, just as sudden premature deaths happen with humans, they also occur in animals.

As it happened, we'd sold her daughter, Daisy-Ella, to another farmer so we didn't have one of her daughters in the herd, but her granddaughter was a few months old. Daisy-Ella-Ella is now two years old and we were delighted when she had a heifer calf this spring. Daisy's heritage will live on in her great granddaughter. Her name? Daisy Della.

Sometimes things happen that make us laugh, even at serious times. When the children were about five and three, I was walking up the yard holding Kate's hand and explaining a sick calf had died and gone to heaven. Will came running down the yard and overheard me.

'He hasn't gone yet,' he called. 'He's still in the shed.'

It's rare we find a cow dead, but it's always horrible when it happens. It's a bolt from the blue; there's worry it will happen again and it stays with you for a while. It can seem strange to non-farmers that people who earn their livelihood sending animals to the factory either when fit for slaughter or in their old age get upset when an animal dies. How can we reconcile sending animals to the factory and then being upset when one dies? It all comes down to being mentally prepared and knowing that our animals are content, well fed and had a good life before going for slaughter in a calm environment. They deserve to live well and it's our responsibility to ensure they do.

One of the more heart-breaking situations that many livestock farmers now face is when their herd is affected by bovine tuberculosis. If animals are found to be infected, they will be slaughtered and the farmer faces being locked up – which means that he or she is unable to sell livestock to other farmers – as well as having animals regularly tested until there are two clear tests in a row. Fourteen of our cows went down with tuberculosis in 1983 but, thankfully, there hasn't been a re-occurrance. To see otherwise-healthy cows walking up the ramp to the slaughterhouse lorry, cows that have been reared since birth on the farm, would bring tears to the eyes of the most hardened of farmers. Unfortunately, it seems to be happening more and more across Ireland, Wales, Scotland and England as efforts seem limited in the attempts to stop it. The annual herd test is always an anxious, stressful time and there's a huge sigh of relief when the 'all clear' is announced for another year.

I think experiencing death and the cycle of life on the farm means farmers can be more accepting of the death of loved ones if it happens in old age. It is recognised that there's a time for human lives to end and living longer wouldn't necessarily provide that person with any quality of life. This is often signalled at wakes and funerals with the lovely expression, 'His work is done' or 'Her work is done.' These gentle words show that every farmer works hard, providing food and looking after the land, but we are only custodians of our farms. We can't bring them with us. We have worked to do our best to improve the farms and hand them on to the next generation. Having lived a good life, there comes a time when we move on and while those left behind will grieve, they also accept it.

THE RUNT OF THE HERD

There's often a runt of the year. Among all the calves born, there is usually one that is so much smaller than the others. In 2015 Becky was the runt. Her mother, grandmother and other ancestors were all fine animals, but she seemed exceptionally small. She has distinctive facial markings; the white stripe down the centre of her face isn't straight but has a few wobbles. She was a fussy feeder and while her comrades were sucking enthusiastically on the teat feeder, I was still feeding her with a bottle so I could check she was getting a full feed. As she matured, she exhibited similar fussiness and stubbornness with anything we asked her to do, be it go into the cattle crush to be dosed or follow the others through a gate to another field. If Becky could be awkward about something, she was.

Her Economic Breeding Index (EBI) score was good, but she wasn't one of our best, so she was marked as one to sell.

When she was a year old, she was included in a group of heifers we were showing to a potential buyer. Brian wondered if she was a bit small.

'She'll make the others look bigger,' was my response. I wasn't overly attached to her and felt there was too much Sixsmith stubbornness in there. Yes, I was having a personality clash with a cow – both of us wanted to be boss. The buyer rejected her on size so she stayed. We didn't mind, we were both intrigued to see if she was going to become a good milking cow.

We didn't get all the cows scanned for pregnancy that year, just the few we weren't sure were pregnant. As Becky's first calving date approached and her belly expanded and swelled, we were convinced she had a monster of a calf in her and were a bit anxious about the impending birth, as she was a bit smaller than her comrades. But in the end she gave birth to a fine set of twins, a bull and a heifer, both small but sturdy and strong, and she joined the milking herd.

She proved to be assertive in the parlour as well, standing her ground against bigger and older cows. She's greedy and likes to be first on a row, believing she gets first choice of the dairy ration served up. Once she has eaten her portion from the manger, she decides she doesn't like being up the front and will poo in protest. Then she gets down on her front knees to see if she can find any spilled ration and will scavenge around in the limited space.

After twins, it can be harder for a cow to go back in calf. Becky seemed to become pregnant at the first attempt and then Brian thought he saw her on heat just as the breeding season had come to an end. He decided not to put the bull to her as it would have been a late calf, but to cull her instead.

However, it must have been just a lively day as we double-checked with a scan, and she is pregnant.

She's a complete pain in the neck at times but we're very glad she is pregnant and will calve soon. Every time I go into the shed she is in, she walks up to the dividing gate. She won't let me stroke her but she'll stand as if she wants to have a chinwag. She's small and feisty. A survivor. Maybe she will mellow with age.

Giving cows a name definitely marks those individuals out as special. Kate names some of the calves, but after a while we struggle to remember them all so she gives up. The names she chooses aren't necessarily short and concise either: we've had Pixie Meadow, Victoria Amelia Hereford, Amelia Jane, Viola Emily, Alexandra, Eustace and and Katie Lou among many others.

WHO'S THE MOTHER SUPERIOR?

Cows are remarkably like humans when it comes to interacting with each other. Call it playground or office politics, but it definitely happens in the field and shed where cows are concerned. Maybe humans are more devious when they bully, and when they want to be the leader who others admire. Cows, though, are very transparent. There are a couple of times of the year when they are split into groups and housed in different sheds. When they come together again, it's easy to spot the signs that they are asserting their rights to be at or near the top of the pecking order. Our cows are divided into three sheds when they come in for the winter. We stop milking them in December to give their bodies time to rest before they calve. This 'dry period' gives their mammary glands time to rejuvenate, lets them put sufficient energy into growing the calf and get in peak condition for giving birth and milking for another ten months.

They are separated into the groups according to their calving dates. As they get closer to calving, they are put into the 'maternity shed' with its deep straw bedding. It houses about twenty cows. As some calves arrive early and some arrive late, the maternity shed can house cows together that are taken from all three sheds. They may not have seen each other for weeks. But even if it is a short gap, as short as two days, they still act like they are complete strangers and will physically fight to decide who is the head honcho. It's usually the older cows who are the matriarchs, the ones who take precedence at the feeding barrier even though there's plenty of room for all, and they'll push their way to their favourite space.

Lucy is thirteen years of age and is the fourth best cow in the herd (based on her EBI score). She's well-built, with a long straight back; a heavy cow with strong shoulders, she plants her hooves firmly on the ground. She never makes a fuss, she never causes aggravation to the person milking. She doesn't get involved in petty bickering nor does she clamour to be first into the milking parlour or first out to grass. While other cows might jostle each other for prime place at the feeding barrier (even though there's very little difference in any places along the row) she doesn't bother. She's often in one of the last rows to be milked but she'll always be the first cow in the row. She never has to be sent in to be milked; she leads the others in. In winter, when they are housed indoors, she asserts her right to a particular cubicle. You'd be forgiven for thinking her name was written up over it, as no other cow gets a look in. The bar on one side is slightly loose, so she is able to push it over and have more room for her large frame. She stands near the gate to the cubicles, and once it is opened she saunters in and doesn't waste any time about lying down. She lets out a huge sigh and looks around as if to say, 'Now that I'm in my favourite armchair, if someone would just bring me a cup of tea, life would be perfect.' It often happens that two of her daughters are standing beside her and they all lie down in a row together. Lucy Mór (Big Lucy) and Lucy Bán (White Lucy) resemble her in size and, when late in pregnancy, they like to take the weight of their hooves after being milked.

Lucy is definitely one of the matriarchs – she doesn't have to bully, she has 'presence'. She just stands firm and flicks her head. Others know not to mess with her. It's as if they know she is mother of Lucifer, our first bull accepted by an A.I. station, and that the humans hugely respect her too. She has four daughters in the milking herd and a number of granddaughters and great-granddaughters. She had another heifer calf last year and hopefully she'll have a couple more.

Last year, a young heifer succeeded in being matriarch of the group of cows in the maternity ward for a short time. It's almost unheard of that such a young cow, barely two years of age, could ascend the pecking order so quickly, but she managed to assert her authority over all the middle-aged cows. They seemed to decide life was too short to fight this little upstart. That was until Lucy went in. She knows she is one of the best cows. She wasn't going to take any cheekiness. She just stood in the middle of the shed, with her hooves firmly planted on the ground and flicked her head. The heifer didn't even try to headbutt her. She recognised Lucy's seniority and capitulated within seconds.

Sometimes we just have to walk away when we put cows into the maternity shed. We can't stand there and watch them headbutt each other, push each other on the shoulders and even occasionally in the stomach, and chase each other around the straw-bedded shed. It's hard to watch knowing that inside those large bodies are soon-to-be-born calves hoping that all stay safe while mothers assert their authority.

THE QUEEN OF THE HERD

There's an old tale about a young man helping his elderly uncle to milk. Noticing an old cow was only being milked on two teats, he queried why she hadn't been culled. If a cow gets mastitis and it isn't caught in time, sometimes she 'loses that quarter', meaning she won't produce milk from that part of the udder. It doesn't necessarily mean she will be culled as a 'three teater' – if she's a good cow she may give as much milk as her comrades, but it is a nail in her coffin. Keeping a 'two teater' would be unheard of in farming circles. The uncle turned to his nephew and said, 'Tha' one's paid a lot o' bills.' That was the end of the discussion: the cow had earned her retirement and was going to get it.

Although many people think that farmers are cruel and ship livestock off to the factory when their useful life has ended, many farm animals enjoy some retirement time. It would be a sad state of affairs if a farmer can't spoil his or her favourite animal in the herd.

Queenie was a special cow and ended her life here in 2015. She had her first calf in 2003, our first calving season on the farm. She came to Brian's attention as a special cow, as she was giving more milk than her herd mates. When we started milk recording, it proved her solids were high too, so she was our star heifer that year. She was a big, strong, square black and white cow with distinctive ears. They were positioned low down; they didn't perk up and looked a little like funnels either side of her head. She had a long white star on her forehead and a white patch above her nose. She always came in early to the parlour. She was reliable and a good milker.

She always calved within the year, even after having twins. She had five sets of twins in total, one of which was heifers, which was a huge bonus. One year, she lay on one of her twins – a bull – and inadvertently killed it. It happens very rarely, but is a risk. Cows are such large animals they don't always notice the little bump under them.

We called her Queenie as she established her position as the best cow and one of the matriarchs in the herd. She had a ritual for establishing her authority. Like Lucy, she didn't need to bully others. She had a presence that they couldn't ignore. When she entered the maternity shed and mixed with cows that hadn't seen each other for a while, she used to walk to the centre of the shed and paw at the straw with her front hooves so that she made a hole down to the concrete. She lowered her knees and rubbed her head in the straw before standing up again to shake her head and perhaps give a bellow. She repeated the process if a few new cows came into the shed. Interestingly, I noticed one of her granddaughters do the very same thing in the maternity shed the other day; she was throwing up so much straw with her head, her back was showered with golden confetti. When the cows went out to grass in the spring, all mixing again as they came from different sheds, Queenie used to repeat the process in the middle of the field, determined to assert her authority for the rest of the milking season.

Queenie was special to us. A cow over fourteen years of age is considered elderly in a commercial herd. The udder is often sagging ponderously; they might have problems with lameness and be unable to walk far. While it would be lovely to give them a nursing home-type retirement in a grassy field and a straw-bedded shed, commercial farmers just wouldn't be able to afford it. Aside from their feed and housing, veterinary bills would increase and there would be a €200 bill to remove her body at the end of her life. Fattened, a good cull cow can make up to €1,000. It may sound harsh to some non-farmers, but the decision comes down to economics at the end of the day.

It's also about acting responsibly and ensuring that they are comfortable, with a good quality of life. Queenie's hooves needed regular attention and she wasn't comfortable walking long distances to the fields furthest from the farmyard. We were beginning to have our doubts about how long we would be able to keep her, but somehow the bull managed to push open the gate to Queenie's shed when she was on heat. Yes, she became pregnant. We then had a valid reason to keep her for another year in the herd, a year where she was going to be spoiled like the queen she was.

If the cows were being grazed in a distant field, Queenie grazed in a nearby paddock with one or two others. When it came time to go indoors for the winter, and most cows were sleeping on relatively comfortable rubber mats on the cubicles, Queenie was in a straw-bedded shed with plenty of comfort. We were concerned she was pregnant with twins again, which we thought would be too much for her, but she had a single calf, a bonny heifer.

Queenie gave eighty thousand kilos of milk in her lifetime.

She gave birth to seven breeding heifers (heifers born in sets of mixed twins are usually infertile). Almost a quarter of the cows in the milking herd are descended from her.

I'm sure sheep farmers would argue there's something special about sheep farming, and so on, but for me there's definitely something special about dairy farming. There's so much satisfaction to be derived from seeing how daughters of your cows turn out, monitoring their progress on a daily basis while milking them, having the statistical information on their milk yields and solids.

Death comes to us all, but it was a sad day when Queenie left us. Just as our heritage will live on in the farm, in the sheds we have built, in the cow tracks we put in, in the flowers and trees we planted, in the land we purchased, Queenie's heritage will live on in the Garrendenny herd through her granddaughters and great-granddaughters, and many descendants into the future.

8

SILAGE MAKING – TRIALS AND TRIBULATIONS

THE TRIALS OF MAKING SILAGE

Livestock are kept in sheds for the winter months. They are protected from the elements, they have plenty of food served up to them every day and the land is protected from damage by their hooves. In the past, cattle were fed on hay, turnips and beet tops.

Although Ireland is wonderfully green, it comes at a price; it gets a lot of rain, so it's not easy to get five dry and sunny days in a row, which is required to make good quality hay. Cut grass and rain don't mix well, especially when farmers are trying to dry it and make nice, sweet-tasting hay.

As farmers looked for a more reliable grass-based winter feed, silage became more popular. Silage is ensiled grass: grass that is cut and stored on a concrete base and under plastic and weights so that air can't get to it, or it is baled and wrapped in polythene. Therefore, it ferments; it dulls in colour but remains nutritious and tasty. Any silage near the edges may go off and will have to be removed but for the most part, silage can last for years as long as it remains covered and airtight. It is much easier to make good silage than it is to make reasonable hay. It's also higher in nutritional value than hay, as the grass is cut at an earlier stage. Ideally, it is cut in dry conditions and left outside in swathes for twenty-four hours to wilt, but if rain is imminent it can be brought to the pit straight away. The harvester collects the mown grass, chops it and blows it into large silage trailers with high sides and a back door that flaps open to discharge the load of cut grass.

The harvesting of silage started in the mid-1950s on this farm, although the first experience couldn't really be described as a success. It's probably best to think of it as a trial run.

Half of High Shores had been planted with barley and the remainder was sown with new grass seeds. Both crops were impressive but there was a problem. How could Dad and Georgie let the cows graze the lush grass and stop them destroying the crop of barley? These were the days before electric fences. Nowadays, a couple of strands of wire with 'pigtail' temporary fence stakes and a battery fencer would do the job of separating the two crops.

The grass was too soft to make hay, so Georgie decided the only solution was to mow the four acres of grass and make silage for the first time. And so they set to work. Once it was mown and had wilted for a day, the two of them started pitching the silage up onto the trailer. It was a nuisance having to stop pitching to move the tractor and trailer frequently so they roped in Herbert, their ten-year-old brother, to drive the tractor. It wasn't the easiest way to learn how to drive, or the calmest. He had to stretch to reach the clutch, so it wasn't the safest of activities either. If he let the clutch out too fast, the tractor skidded and damaged the freshly reseeded ground. Then he'd hear a shout from Georgie berating him for not doing it properly.

The sun beat down on this beautiful July day – it was perfect silage-making weather. The field was set high on the farm and sloped downwards. Therefore, they were visible to all neighbours and road users in nearby Crettyard. All and sundry could see the three Sixsmith lads out making their first-ever crop of silage. Even today, silage-making is a major topic of conversation among farmers. Who has it cut already? Who got caught with rain? Who has a 'savage cut' (high in volume but not necessarily good in quality)? Who is steeped in luck because they got it cut, drawn in and covered just before it rained?

Georgie and Dad were using the famous non-tipping trailer so they had to fork all the silage out again once they drove it down to the yard. They didn't have a concrete base so they forked it onto clay. Neither did they have a clamp or polythene, so there was no way of eliminating air from it. So the four acres of cut grass sat there in a huge pile, taunting them while it rotted slowly until it was mixed with dung and spread on the land. All in the name of experimentation, I guess.

They didn't make silage again for over a decade. In 1969, Dad was mowing High Shores with a tractor-drawn forage harvester and was tipping the loads of cut grass outside the pit. Tommy was driving the other tractor and using the buckrake to lift and push the grass into the pit and a neighbour, Harold, was spreading it out with a pitchfork. They swapped when Tommy decided Harold wasn't working fast enough. As Harold reversed, a back wheel of the tractor went up on the mound of silage, the tractor started to tip to the side and it kept tipping until it had fallen over completely. Luckily the tractor had a cab – many didn't at that time – and Harold was able to crawl out. 'Quick, help me turn it back up before he comes back,' he said, trying to lift it with his bare hands as though he was trying to right a wheelbarrow.

Dad was driving down the hill from High Shores and had seen it all happen, the wheels going up in the air as if in slow motion. He was so relieved to see everyone was safe and little damage done that there wasn't much said at all. As they were working to fix the buckrake, Mum came out to tell Dad to go in and shower, they'd be heading to the hospital soon. I was born the next day.

MEMORIES OF MAKING SILAGE

In the early 1970s, Dad started getting a contractor to cut the silage and built two more silage pits. One hundred acres of grass can be drawn in within a single day now. In the 1970s and 1980s, it took over a week. The trailers were much smaller and the machinery for pushing the fresh grass into the pit was much slower and less powerful. It was much more labour intensive too. As well as the contractors and Tommy, a couple of neighbours always came to work for a few days. Retired from working in the mines or as farm labourers elsewhere, often with a small farm and cattle of their own, these were always lithe men, never tall but strong and supple, retaining some fitness from their days of playing amateur Gaelic football. Two men had the job of forking the silage around so it spread evenly in the pit and another two tractor drivers were driving to and fro over the silage multiple times to compress it down as tightly as possible.

My earliest silage memory is of a near accident. As our yard is on a steep slope, the sheds and silage pit are built on different levels. The tractor drivers reversed at the top yard and tipped the load of grass over the edge so it landed neatly in front of the silage pit eight feet below. Richard, one of the contractors, was sixteen at the time, and I was about four. Richard reversed, the trailer started to tip up but the silage was tight in the trailer and wasn't coming out as normal. The weight of the trapped silage lifted the axle. Then the drawbar of the trailer lifted the tractor by the back wheels. As the brakes were on the back wheels, they weren't able to work. The trailer started to slide back and pulled the tractor back along with it. The trailer fell off the edge, pulling the tractor further back. Luckily, the trailer partially rested on some unloaded silage, didn't fall to the side and the tractor stopped, just a couple of feet from the edge of the top yard. The men worked furiously with their pitchforks to empty the trailer while Richard was sitting nearby, pretending he was fine, but even at the age of four I sensed how terrifying it must have been to experience your tractor being pulled back towards a deep abyss while being powerless to stop it.

Some years later, there was a near tractor crash on the avenue during the silage harvesting. Young men on their summer holidays were driving for the contractor, and some had friends on the tractors as passengers. There was no such thing then as leaving doors on tractors and quite often the tarpaulin roofs on old tractors were removed too. No one worried about sunburn or farmers' tans and they could exchange banter when tractors met each other along the four-mile round trip between the home yard and the outfarm. Although the tractor drivers weren't having races, they seemed to be determined to gain ground on each other, egged on by their passengers.

It was a humid and balmy summer's evening and it was getting close to midnight, so it was almost completely dark. One driver, halfway up our narrow avenue to the yard, realised he was out of diesel when his tractor stopped suddenly. He switched off the lights to save his battery while attempting to restart and get to the yard. Another driver, going down the avenue, was only a few feet from him when he saw the lights glimmer on. His only option to prevent a crash was to career off into the field to the left, trying to steer between the concrete stakes and newly planted trees along a downward slope. He then yanked the steering wheel to the right so managed to rejoin the avenue once clear of the halted tractor. No damage was done except one concrete post and a couple of newly planted trees were taken out. They came back to repair it the next day.

Sometimes I wonder that for every accident that causes injury, how many near misses happen? The tractor that ran out of diesel and stopped, by the way, was made in 1968 and is still going strong; it's enjoying a leisurely retirement being driven in vintage tractor runs.

PRE-SILAGE TENSION

Breakdowns seemed to happen frequently then. A single tractor or trailer breakdown wasn't a huge problem, but if something happened to the forage harvester, everything had to stop. One day, the men had just finished their dinner and were working only five minutes when the harvester broke down. They all sat on the garden wall for four hours while it was being repaired, and then it wasn't worthwhile getting started as it was teatime, so they trooped back in for their tea. I have to admit that if that happened now and I was cooking tea, I'd insist on some work being done first or I'd package up the sandwiches and let them eat while driving the tractors! I've an unwritten rule: people have to earn their supper before they get a cooked meal – well, nearly always. Bad weather and breakdowns really increased the tension. Silage is an expensive crop to harvest and if the quality wasn't good then the livestock would need a supplement of expensive ration during the winter. Delays meant the farmer was stressed just by looking at the weather forecast and the sky. The contractor would be trying to appear relaxed to give the impression everything was under control and his next clients might arrive in the field wondering when he was going to arrive at his farm. It wasn't easy to keep everyone happy. The farm wife was probably sick to the back teeth of feeding eight hungry men three meals a day for a week and would be glad to see the back of them.

We always wanted to stay up late, to still be up when men came in for their supper, but we had to go to bed even though we were convinced we'd never sleep. Our bedrooms were filled with the scent of cut grass and the headlights of tractors filtered in through the curtains as they drove up and down. But in the end the trundle of the trailers, followed by the deep voices of men as they came in for their supper, lulled us to sleep.

Advances in technology mean that rather than having to get a few neighbours to come and help, Brian doesn't have much to do beyond being there should they need an opinion on anything. Silage tends to be cut earlier now too, six weeks after the application of fertiliser, with the second cut six weeks after that again. Some farmers still prefer quantity to quality, letting the grass grow for eight or more weeks instead of six, letting it bulk up and shoot out so they can say they got a 'savage cut of silage', having more in the pit but of lower quality. It can be stressful – getting the weather forecast wrong can make incorrect timing an expensive mistake. Many farming families suffer from 'Pre-Silage Tension'. Once one neighbour makes a move and starts mowing the grass, this can increase anxiety among others, especially if the weather is unsettled. Should they risk it or should they wait? Even the calmest of farmers will experience twinges of PST. It's a case of keeping your head down, an eye on the weather forecast and investing in large bars of chocolate to calm the nerves.

I'm often surprised by the number of people who go and watch silage being cut and harvested. Farmers don't like to sit inside on a warm summer's evening, so popping along to have a look at the yield and the quality of someone else's silage is relaxing entertainment. Of course, the farmer who owns the land knows their silage will be assessed, cogitated over and discussed at length, so this can increase the stress levels if things aren't going to plan. I went over with a picnic tea to the person mowing one evening and I was trying to work out why there were at least half a dozen Jeeps and cars in the Top Field, men and lads all standing around and watching him mow. I hadn't noticed that instead of the usual front and back mower, which cut two widths of grass, this new mower was cutting three and then it was putting all three cuts into one large swathe. Just as people once went to watch the first binders and harvesters, this butterfly mower was attracting considerable attention. I'm not the least bit interested in machinery, so I really couldn't see what all the fuss was about.

The day after the harvesting of the silage holds the most work for the farming family. The silage pit has to be covered with polythene. No one comes to watch that, as they'd get roped in to help. The whole family gets involved, particularly if there's a breeze. Bodies are needed to stand on the huge rectangle of black polythene when it is unfolded and pulled into place, which is easier said than done. I struggle with covering a dish with cling film so covering a pit of forty by one hundred feet is definitely not my forte. The polythene used to be held in place with a layer of dung, which was rather a messy and unpleasant procedure. Thankfully, old tyres are now used instead. This provides a great workout, and it's quite satisfying to hurl tyres around. In some ways, there's more camaraderie on the silage-covering day, as a couple of the contractors come back to help, so there's plenty of chat up on top of the silage.

AN ARMY MARCHES ON ITS STOMACH

The silage week was a long one for farm wives. Their role was to prepare three meals a day for the men: dinner, tea and supper. The largest meal of the day, dinner, was eaten at 1 p.m. on most farms. The men trooped in for their dinner of meat, two vegetables and floury potatoes. Dessert was homemade: rhubarb tart, rice pudding or a steamed pudding. Big mugs of tea were accompanied by queen cakes or biscuit cake. Tea for the contractors was usually a meal of sausages, rashers, mushrooms, baked beans and fried eggs, or sandwiches if they were eating in the silage field. Supper, served around

Memories of a farming family – Dad is the baby here! 1939.

Playtime in the barn, 1939.

Dressed in his best. Dad, circa 1948.

Dad, his parents and siblings, circa 1948.

George and Lily at
the back door of
Garrendenny Castle,
1950s.

Growing up on the
farm. Lorna, aged
ten months, with
Dad, June 1970.

Lorna's godfather,
Cecil Mills, aged two,
with his mother Evelyn
(Lily's sister), outside
Garrendenny Castle,
1949.

Dad with Pupsy and
Rover, 1968.

Life is good ... Lorna with
Mum, 1971.

Dressed for herding. Lorna with
Dad and Pupsy in Doonane, 1972.

In the cab of a Massey Ferguson. Lorna with Tommy Byrne, our workman for over twenty years, 1972.

No driving licence needed. Lorna, 1972.

Great-uncle Bob Agar leading Lorna on her first pony, 1982.

Dad demonstrates how to ride bareback on Lucy, 1982.

Al fresco dining with silage contractors, 1980. Lorna, Daphne and Alden are in the background.

Fashion forward, 1980.

Kate with her pet lamb, Matilda, who went on to have many sets of triplets, rearing them all herself, 2008.

All set for a Sunday cycle, 1980s-style – Lorna, Daphne, Alden and Dad.

Never too young! Will and Kate move cattle from one field to another in Doonane, 2009.

Will and Kate bring cows to be milked from the Bog, 2013.

Not as easy as it looks. The goats are put to bed and Becky is as awkward as ever, 2009.

Sam hard at work bringing in the cows from the Letterbox field.

Pleased as punch.
Will with lamb,
2014.

Will and Kate on a bright day on Garrendenny Lane.

Will learns how to milk, 2014.

Under the greenwood tree. Kate with Lou, 2016.

In the milking parlour, 2016.

Nothing at all to see here, 2016.

Bringing the cows home. Kate, 2016.

Kate, farming's new generation.

A farmer's best friends. Lorna with Lou and Sam, 2017.

Family with cows, 2017.

11 p.m. was more sandwiches with scones, spotted dick or queen cakes to follow.

Given the fragmented nature of many of Ireland's farms, meals often had to be packed up and transported to whichever field the workers were in. Mum served dinners of meat, potatoes and vegetables into hot Pyrex dishes, each one covered with a lid and wrapped in a tea towel before being stored in a box, all packed in tightly so they wouldn't budge. A big saucepan of rice pudding, bowls and spoons were in another box, and a third held mugs, teaspoons, milk, sugar and flasks of tea with a tin of freshly baked queen cakes.

When we arrived at the yellow field with its dark green swathes of cut grass, men continued working until half of the dinner was unpacked and then ambled over. Picnic rugs were never used. Picnic baskets didn't make an appearance either. Men kneeled on the ground or sat on an upturned bucket or an old tyre, all in a semicircle, while Mum served everything out from the boot of the car. We insisted on having our dinners from mini Pyrex dishes, but once we'd eaten we got bored listening to the chat and ran off to practise our long jumps over the swathes, enjoying the smell of the sun-warmed grass and plunging our hands into the coolness of the swathe. If the sun was shining and the weather forecast was good, the men were relaxed and took their time over their tea and cake. There was no rush to get to the next farm; they knew they'd be working late and they needed a break. Lots of banter was exchanged as well as local farming news. If clouds were threatening, they ate quickly and went straight back to their tractors. We helped Mum to pack up all the dirty dishes. Then there was the fun of going home to stack the dishwasher, put a cake in the oven and start making sandwiches for the tea.

Making the sandwiches was organised like a military operation on the kitchen table. Sliced pans of white bread were buttered first. There was no point in buttering wholemeal bread; they'd all be left uneaten. The butter had been left out of the refrigerator so it would be soft and spreadable. My sister Daphne and I had the task of buttering bread. We took two slices at a time, laid them side by side, buttered them both and then sandwiched them together, adding them to a teetering pile from where Mum took them to add sandwich fillings.

Egg salad sandwiches have always been a firm favourite. There is much store in a good egg salad sandwich and it's important to get it right. I've overheard women at wakes comparing notes. It all comes down to the proportion of egg to tomatoes to lettuce, and not letting juice from the tomatoes into the mixture or it goes soggy. Some prefer salad cream, others prefer mayonnaise. Some consider diced onion or scallions to be essential, others wouldn't include them at all. The good news is that as long as they are served in white bread and aren't soggy, the silage contractors don't seem to be too fussy.

Many farm women work off farm now, so some silage contractors bring their own meals with them. Around here, most farmers still feed the contractors, but the good news is that it is usually all done and dusted in a day. Sometimes I even escape with only having to serve up one or two meals. And they tend to come to the house for it, so gone are the days of bringing food to the field.

THE STRANGER IN THE MIDST

Hospitality was taken very seriously by many farm families and refusing hospitality could offend. Expressions like 'the kettle is always on', 'sure, you'll have a bit of dinner' and 'sit down there and pull up a chair' meant you'd leave the table half a stone heavier. One day, Dad was helping a neighbour with the threshing, but he left without having the teatime meal as he knew his fourteen cows were waiting to be hand-milked and other family members were away. When he met the neighbour at another threshing the next day, he discovered that his absence had been noticed and he had to promise never to do such a thing again. The family had been appalled at teatime when it was discovered that my dad had gone home without anything to eat.

It was with this heritage of hospitality in mind that I returned to farming with some trepidation in 2002 at the age of thirty-three. Having to cook almost every meal was a huge consideration in our decision to return to farming – at least for me. When we worked nine-to-five, Brian did most of the cooking, and if we had dinner parties he planned the menu and cooked while I chopped vegetables, set the table, arranged flowers and washed up. I wasn't convinced that my cooking skills were up to the challenge of satisfying silage contractors – men who claim they will eat anything yet can be surprisingly fussy. I also knew that while my English friends were appreciative of a shop-bought biscuit with a cup of tea, home baking would be expected in Ireland. Rural women were expected to bake for all kinds of functions and it was almost essential to have something home-baked on the chance someone called in. God forbid you had to offer them a Rich Tea biscuit.

I was relatively pleased with my preparations for feeding the contractors for the first time. I had three chicken casseroles in the oven, so even if they were late for dinner there was no risk of the meat drying out, and bowls of new floury potatoes were keeping warm. The kitchen table had been extended and was set for ten places, although I was unsure how many men would be coming in. My mother had often fed the contractors' sons too, if any of them were on the tractors. I wasn't so sure I was up to the challenge of feeding children as well as men.

It is rare that the first silage man to arrive back in the yard will come into the kitchen on his own. Shy or feeling safer in numbers, he will wait for other tractors to arrive so three or four arrive together, throwing off boots at the back door in deference to a supposedly clean kitchen floor. I have a long pew at the back of my kitchen table, perfect for seating six or seven small children at a birthday party tea. These grown men looked a bit uncertain as three of them squeezed in to sit on it – maybe they thought I would get them to say a prayer – and mumbled a thank you as I placed plates of chicken casserole in front of them.

I wasn't sure whether the flicker of relief washing over their faces meant they were happy it looked edible or they were glad their next meal here wouldn't be for a few months. They seemed pleased with the new potatoes in any case, as the skins fell away and their flouriness was soaked up by the gravy.

I was about to offer seconds when Dad walked in with a young man I hadn't seen before. Sometimes the contractors have sons with them or young lads on their school holidays driving the tractors, so I nodded at them to take their seats and served up two more plates. The young man's blue eyes widened as he looked at the plate of food.

'Is that for me?' he asked.

'Yes,' I replied somewhat surprised and, as an afterthought, I added, 'Enjoy.'

He did. He tucked in with gusto and a smile on his face.

I cleared away plates, making a mental note to be less generous with the vegetables in the casseroles the next time. Some left carrots and some didn't like mushrooms, but the peas and onions seemed to be popular.

I noticed the young man had cleared his plate.

As I served rhubarb crumble and hot custard, the men started chatting. With bellies full, their tongues and brains could work in tandem, so they compared notes and news. As the pudding bowl was placed in front of each man, he glanced at it as if suspicious of the contents and then relaxed slightly.

All except the young guy: his eyes widened further and his mouth broke into a wide grin as he tucked in. Perhaps he was the silent type, I thought, as I scalded the large teapot. None of the other men seemed to be talking to him, whereas they usually teased children and teenagers. However, he seemed happy enough as he drank tea and ate slices of biscuit cake.

As they supped the last dregs of tea from the mugs, the driver of the harvester stood up – the signal their dinner break was over. The men got to their feet and grunted a thank you as they went out.

The teenager smiled and thanked me profusely. If he was a new member of staff, I hoped his enthusiasm would rub off on the others in time.

There was no sign of the lad at teatime. The men seemed

pleased that I was serving up a fry of sausages, rashers and eggs with baked beans – not a vegetable in sight.

'Where's the young blond lad?' I enquired.

No one knew. Nor did any of them know who he was. It turned out he had walked down to where they were cutting silage on the outfarm. A teenager, bored and on his summer holidays, he'd asked for a jaunt on a tractor and the driver had left him sitting on it when going in for dinner. When Dad saw him sitting there he insisted that he come in for a bit of dinner. Never could a person be left in the yard while dinner was being served inside. The rest of the contractors, seeing him come in with my dad, had presumed he was a visitor of ours. After they had finished drawing in silage from the outfarm, he had headed home.

To this day, I still don't know who it was that sat at my dinner table that hot summer's day and tucked into my cooking like it was the best he had ever tasted.

9

SUNDAYS PAST AND PRESENT

A DAY OF REST

In the 1940s and 1950s, unnecessary work on a Sunday wasn't just disapproved of, it wasn't permitted. The Sixsmiths weren't as strict as some households, where Sunday dinner was served cold, cooked the day before. My grandmother Lily didn't go to church; she had to stay at home to keep the fire going in the range and cook the dinner. She sang hymns as she worked and I'm sure she enjoyed the peace and quiet when everyone else was out of the house.

In terms of farm work, the cows were milked and all animals were fed and watered, but that was it. My grandfather probably interpreted the importance of it being a day of rest more seriously than some neighbouring farmers. If they were delivering milk to the creamery on a Sunday morning, they had to milk the cows an hour earlier than normal. Rather than do that, my grandparents stayed in bed and milked later. They made butter from Sunday's milk and sold it in a shop in Carlow, even though it would have been more lucrative to have delivered the milk to the creamery.

Even if rain threatened during the harvest, they still didn't work on Sundays. One year, the weather had been changeable. There were a couple of fine days and they got the wheat cut. It was too wet to bring to the shed in case it heated, so the sheaves were stacked in stooks in the field for a few days. However, the forecast promised heavy rain on the Monday and they wanted to get the stooks in before they got wet again. The family spent the Sunday as normal: went to church, chatted to visitors, milked the cows, had tea and then sat in the kitchen until midnight. At one minute past midnight, under the harvest moon, George and his two sons, my dad and Georgie, went out with the horse and haycart to bring the stooks to the hayshed in preparation for the threshing on another day. They finished up as the sun was rising. And yes, it did rain that morning, so they felt their efforts were rewarded.

On another occasion, a contractor was cutting their wheat and didn't get it finished on the Saturday evening. 'I'll come back and finish it in the morning,' he said. George nearly had a fit and insisted he didn't return until the Monday. He decided then and there that if he had to beg, borrow or steal, he would have his own binder for the following year.

A neighbour came up on a Saturday evening to ask to borrow the paddy rake, which was used to make haycocks, and George gave it to him. His elderly father was cross with him for lending it. Not because he didn't want the neighbour to have it, but because he knew they'd be working on the Sunday. He argued, 'They t'ink they 'ave us codded, ya shouldn't have given it to 'em.'

SUNDAY SOCIALISING

Sunday was a very sociable day for Dad and his siblings, even though they only went to church and usually spent the rest of the day at home. All baking was done on the Saturday in the knowledge that lots of visitors would be calling up. This included brown bread, spotted dick, eight apple tarts and ginger bread. Not a crumb was left by Sunday evening. Granny's sister Pansy and her husband called regularly. Their sister Charlotte from England came over for holidays with her daughter every summer. Other siblings visited occasionally. Neighbours often mentioned to Grandad after church that they'd be out for a drive after dinner and would call up. When Dad's older sisters went out to work in shops or got married, they visited with boyfriends and husbands.

The highlight of Sunday was a visit from Uncle Charlie. He was Grandad's brother and in many ways they were like chalk and cheese. George wasn't that mechanically minded, he never took to tractors and always preferred the days of the horse and plough. He drove his black Ford car very slowly for the weekly visits to town, at a maximum of thirty miles per hour. Charlie, however, owned a black open-top two-seater Riley sports car and he drove it as fast as it would go. Young neighbouring lads used to lie in wait for him on Sundays for the thrill of watching him fly past them, his white hair blowing back with the wind. There weren't speedometers in cars then, so he used a stopwatch to time himself driving the ten miles from Carlow to Garrendenny, trying to beat his best time each week.

When petrol was in short supply during the war, Charlie traded in his car and bought a motorbike. Crashing at speed one day, he ended up in hospital in Dublin for a couple of weeks. On getting out of hospital, he went straight to a garage to buy another motorbike and he drove it home.

He was eccentric but relaxed. Charlie had a shop where he sold and repaired radios and charged batteries for people in the pre-electricity days when radios needed wet and dry batteries. He lived in a flat above the shop and ate in a local café for every meal. He didn't even have a kettle to make a cup of tea. He wasn't an early riser and his assistant knew to tell early callers that he was out on a job rather than asleep upstairs.

He visited Garrendenny almost every Sunday. Occasionally he was invited to visit other relatives but, although he went, he complained about having to go. He enjoyed the relaxation of Garrendenny. During the summer, he'd call up at least one evening a week. He and George sat in the field outside the garden, where our house is located now, and they'd watch the world go by.

He always brought treats. He'd have brought a bar of chocolate for each child every Sunday and three-quarters of a pound of sweets to be shared out. He brought an extra bar of chocolate for whichever of Dad's sisters had washed and ironed his shirts from the previous week. When the children were young, they all had to go indoors when he arrived while he hid the sweets and chocolate bars among the shrubs in the large front garden. The weekly treasure hunt created huge excitement. Never was a chocolate bar left behind, undiscovered.

After the cows were milked and the tea of sandwiches and cake was devoured, most of the family and visitors retired to the sitting room, but George and Charlie used to stay in the kitchen, smoking and having their own chat. Sometimes they were joined by Pat, the workman, before he went off to play cards in a neighbour's house. Charlie was also interested in horses and the three of them used to have lengthy chats about ploughing.

SUNDAYS IN THE 1970s

Brian and I had similar experiences of Sundays as children, which isn't that surprising given we're of the same religion and both from farming backgrounds. The preparation for Sunday started the previous evening. Potatoes were scrubbed, vegetables prepared, a dessert was made, shoes polished, Sunday clothes checked and children washed. Sunday morning involved the usual jobs of milking cows and herding, followed by the family excursion to church. Church was a lengthy affair then.

We had to arrive early, as Mum played the music. I don't mean she played the organ, we didn't have an organist in our parish, but we had a record player so she needed a few minutes to find the chosen hymns. The men always went to the shed for a chat, waiting until the bell had stopped ringing before going indoors to take their places at the edge of their family pews.

After the service, the men returned to the shed to resume their farming conversations, which normally lasted for half an hour or more. The women, often with little in common beyond having married farmers in the area, stood in the tiny porch and made conversation. The children played in the graveyard, exploring the graves with railings around them, particularly enjoying the sense of darkness and horror amid the yew hedging within. Garrendenny Lane started at the church gate, so sometimes we walked a little way along it and played at jumping back and forth across the stream. Jumping across one way was easy, as the lane was higher than the opposite bank, but jumping back was more of a challenge. One time my sister Daphne missed her footing and landed in the middle of the stream, her white sandals and socks soaked and muddy.

After church, we drove to Castlecomer to get the Sunday papers. We got our comics – *Beano, Twinkle* and *Bunty*. There were usually a few bars of chocolate or packets of sweets put into the bag. Sunday lunch was roast chicken, beef or lamb. If the Sunday was wet or wintry and we were staying at home, we spent the afternoon in front of the fire reading and watching television, perhaps playing cards or a board game. Afternoon tea was usually eaten in front of the fire before Dad headed out again to the evening milking or to check on the livestock.

Sundays often involved visitors. As our parents came from big families, there was a host of aunts, uncles and cousins to see. My paternal grandmother and great-aunts came quite often. Mum collected them in Carlow and dropped them off at church before returning to the house to collect us. All were tall, upright, grey-haired ladies who carried massive black handbags and retained the habit of wearing a hat to church. My afternoon was spent buried among the pages of my latest Enid Blyton or Hardy Boys book while they caught up on the news of pregnancies, weddings (shotgun ones were preferred), births and deaths, with the occasional relative's achievement thrown in for good measure. I think one of the reasons I decided to keep my own name on getting married was I had developed a subconscious horror of ever being described by old ladies as 'she used to be a Sixsmith'. It frequently happened that one or other aunt wouldn't recognise a name and the storyteller had to recall the woman's maiden name. Of course, I'm probably described as 'that strange one that's still a Sixsmith', but that will do.

The autumn was a particularly busy time for visits to relatives and for receiving them back. Farm work was easing and people often attended the afternoon Harvest Thanksgiving service in another parish. They then went to relatives or friends in that parish for tea, where they would discuss the choice of hymns, the guest preacher, the quality of the singing, and any news they heard after the service. Many visits were to aunts and uncles who had children, so we had good fun playing. If they didn't have children our age it was an extremely boring afternoon, but life became much better when I was allowed to bring a book and read in peace in a world of my own.

Doing unnecessary work on a Sunday was still frowned upon in the 1970s and 1980s. For example, if it was 'your month' to put flowers in the church, they couldn't be arranged and delivered on a Sunday morning. That had to be done on the Saturday. I remember asking to be allowed to knit on a Sunday, arguing that one woman in *The Riordans* – shown on a Sunday around 6.30 p.m. – knitted furiously for most of the programme.

Once a year, we attended the local sports day in the priest's field within view of our house. The excitement built as we saw stalls being set up and cars arriving. The highlight for me was always the bottle stall, where we swapped ten pence for a chance to win a bottle of orange, a bar of soap or that elusive prize of a giant teddy or something similar. I remember winning a bottle of beer and insisting on delivering it to Tommy that evening, as my parents didn't drink alcohol and I was sure Tommy would enjoy it. Daphne won a packet of stock cubes and we didn't know what they were, opening up one to see what it was like. Women wearing headscarves stood outside the roped barrier, exchanging pound notes for numerous tickets. As the evening wore on, there were chances of getting even more tickets for your pound if the crowd had been smaller than usual or people had spent less. Each ticket was unfurled carefully and examined before either being discarded or gleefully handed back in. All watched to see what the next prize was and who it was going to.

We went through to the other field for the amusement rides and we peeked at the football match before losing interest quite quickly. We persuaded Dad to enter the fathers' race one year and lost sight of him in the throng as lots of men were fitter and faster and quite competitive. He thought he came third last but didn't stick around to find out. Dad always reminded us that he and his siblings were never allowed to attend this sports day – it wasn't done to go out in public to such an event on a Sunday.

Sometimes we went for a cycle on Sunday afternoons. I think we were considered quite eccentric for doing such a thing. Around here, people still viewed the bicycle as a mode of transport rather than for use as a leisure pursuit. How times have changed, as most Sundays now we see bunches of cyclists passing the gate in their colourful Lycra gear.

SUNDAYS CHANGING

I noticed Sundays changing when shops began to open seven days a week. In 1994, when I was at university and living in Salisbury, I got a job in the local Sainsbury's on Sunday mornings. I worked for four hours and the supermarkets could only open for six hours.

But work on a Sunday is inevitable for farmers. At busy times of the year, the number of hours off is limited to two or three before the evening milking has to be done. If it's a busy day of cows calving, there isn't even time to sit down in front of the fire. On the very rare occasion we go shopping on a Sunday, I'm always struck by how busy it is and how shopping is now entertainment. As a reluctant shopper, I can't imagine anything worse; necessary farm work on a Sunday doesn't seem too bad in comparison. Popular days out for farming families, of course, are the agricultural shows, held on summer Sundays, and we always go to the couple of local ones.

My favourite Sunday activities are a family trip to the beach or to Altamont Gardens or Duckett's Grove in summer, or a lazy afternoon with a book by the fire in winter. The cows still have to be milked on Sunday evenings, but our cows are as relaxed about timekeeping as we are! While many cows adhere to a strict routine, ours have learned to stay grazing or lying down until they see us coming to get them. It's very rare that they queue at the gate.

Like many others, Sunday for us is a day to recharge the batteries, rejuvenate the body for the week ahead and catch up on family time.

10

CURES – DO THEY WORK?

Cures were part and parcel of growing up in Ireland. Neighbours talked of going to bone setters for dislocated bones or sprains, people visited my grandmother to get a cure for wetting the bed (a drink that tasted disgusting apparently), and as I had severe eczema and medical treatment by doctors was limited in its effectiveness, we visited various 'quacks' for cures. A cure was usually passed down from parent to child, either in terms of having the gift of curing or the method of making up a medicine or ointment.

Healers existed for various complaints such as shingles, colic, sprains, warts, heart conditions, epilepsy, ringworm, asthma and more. Sometimes the afflicted person would write to or phone the healer to request being included in a prayer, but more often than not they had to visit the healer. One of the more memorable cures for my eczema involved having sticky tar-like ointment plastered on my limbs and covered with bandages. As part of that cure, I also drank concoctions that resembled watered-down stewed rhubarb and tasted revolting. In fairness, they did help but didn't eliminate the eczema completely. One cure we tried didn't involve taking any dubious substances; we just had to say the rosary in the house of the healer. However, we are Church of Ireland. Our only experience of the rosary was hearing it at the occasional funeral. The lady didn't say the rosary with us but left us the rosary beads and a booklet with the prayers written out. We started, and after some time, she rejoined us, expecting us to be finished, but we were only halfway through. Off she went, convinced not only were we heathens but we were dim heathens. Didn't we realise it could be recited at speed?

At long last we were almost finished when she returned again and, as she sat there to listen to us say prayers on the last beads, she realised why it had taken us so long. We had said the Creed too many times.

'Maybe it will work extra well,' my mother said with some effort at positivity. The woman didn't look convinced but said it might. It was clear from her expression she thought we'd be in limbo forever rather than being granted a cure.

At that stage, I had just a few small patches of eczema on my legs. Within two weeks, the rash had spread up my legs, from ankle to knee. It was one thing for a cure to fail, but to make things worse didn't go down well.

A man from Tullow provided the most successful cure. He was able to establish what foods I was allergic to by holding my hand and seeing if a brass pendulum would sway when held over the names of various foodstuffs. It swung like anything over 'cow's milk' as well as other dairy products. Yes, I recognised the irony even then. When we moved up to live in Garrendenny in 2005 – we lived off-farm for the first three years – my eczema flared up terribly. Someone mentioned that the gentleman, although very elderly, still saw people on occasion. I discovered I was still allergic to all the previous foodstuffs, but gluten was now causing me problems too. But the biggest culprit was all the pine trees planted around the house. We had planned to cut them down, but it became a priority. And, yes, it worked.

It's easy to understand the popularity of cures in the nineteenth and twentieth centuries, as attending a doctor was expensive and many people didn't have transport to get to a town. Medical science has improved, but many of the old cures are still used. Neighbours afflicted with shingles visit an old lady who says a prayer over them to cure it. When the children were toddlers and were showing signs of having allergies, I brought them to a kineaologist, a cranial osteopath and to a healer who simply rubbed at a specific area on their backs. The healer had the longest waiting list and the fullest waiting room. Did it work? It definitely helped.

Local remedies and cures were used on livestock too. Apart from the cost of calling out a vet, any reader of the James Herriot books knows their medical resources were limited before the 1950s. One of the more serious illnesses that affected cattle was blood murrain, now known as Redwater. It could kill cattle if it wasn't spotted quickly. It is a parasitic infection spread by ticks in long grass and bracken. It occurs much less frequently now, as grass is kept short and managed more effectively. Signs were blood in the urine, diarrhoea and then constipation. Dad lost a cow to it once. There were four dry cows down in Byrne's Bog and, when herding one day, there was a sudden downpour so he just had a quick look at them. The next day it was late when he did the herding and the damage was done. A locally recommended cure was to give them a drink of their own urine and two pints of stout. Other suggested cures included dosing the animal with buttermilk and turpentine, strong tea or treacle and Epsom salts.

Of course, many diseases that killed animals or affected their development and well-being are now easily prevented by vaccines or regular dosing with products that kill parasites such as liver fluke or stomach worms.

A holy well is located in the graveyard at Kilgorey, within a mile of our house as the crow flies. It dates from AD 550 when a monastery was built there. In penal times – when Roman Catholics weren't allowed to worship – it was used as a Mass station. It was reported that water flowed from a hole six feet high in a tree trunk there and the holy well was a place of pilgrimage for centuries. It was believed that dipping a strip of the afflicted person's clothing into the well water and then tying it to a nearby hawthorn tree transferred the infirmity away from the person and onto the living shrubbery; and so, hoping for a cure to work, people tied scraps of their clothing to trees and bushes near the well.

Kilgorey Well was supposed to be effective in curing lameness. One story reports that a woman visited the well with her lame son on three successive mornings before sunrise, and on the third morning he was able to walk.

Strange occurrences happened too. Once, when people were working in nearby Agar's Bog harvesting turf, one person visited the well to get water to make tea. It was reported that, try as they may, they could not get the water to reach the boil, a sure sign that the well had the power to cure.

Today the graveyard is accessed via a lane. It was renovated in the 1950s and it is well kept; some gravestones have been renovated and the outline of the ancient monastery is marked by low walls, so people can stand or sit within the confines of the original building. Walls have been built around the altar and shrine so older people can sit in some comfort sheltered against the wind during the annual service in May.

The gravestones show details of burials from the 1760s. It is rare anyone is buried there now, but there have been two burials in the last five years. It's a beautiful place to be buried, even if in practical terms, when one is six foot under, it's not possible to see the colourful patchwork of fields all around, feel the wind blowing or hear the birdsong.

11

A FARMER'S BEST FRIEND

Farm dogs, in our experience, tend to either be very good or absolutely terrible at working cattle – always one extreme or the other. The first dog they brought to Garrendenny was only a pet, completely useless at rounding up cattle or sheep.

A couple of years after arriving in Garrendenny, when collecting the newspaper from the letterbox one day, Dad met a man who asked if they'd be interested in a pup. He said they would and a couple of days later the man arrived with a black and white collie. He was given the creative name of Pupsy and turned out to be a good worker. His only flaw was if he saw something happen that he interpreted to mean 'home time for cows' – perhaps the closing of a particular gate – he'd shoot off to bring in the cows, perhaps two hours earlier than normal.

In the mid-1960s, Dad got another pup and he was named Pupsy too. He was a typical black and white collie, quite large for the breed, long-haired and silky. This dog was a very skilled and reliable worker. He went for the cows when told to do so. He loved jumping into the boot of the car and going over to the outfarm, where he rounded up cattle, if required, or just walked along quietly when herding. He didn't display any jealousy when I was born. When I was sleeping in my pram in the garden, he used to lie under it and saw his role as a protector. Not that there were many callers, but only family, the postman and our workman were allowed near that pram when I was in it.

He was killed on the road when I was four and he was nine. There was a bad thunderstorm while Mum and Dad were at a dinner dance, and the babysitter didn't know he was normally allowed indoors during a storm. He ran off and was hit by a car. It was two days later before they found his body in a ditch, after walking the fields for miles calling and searching.

His brilliance became more apparent, as it was decades before we got a dog as good again. We did buy a partially trained one-year-old collie, who was shaping up to be a skilled dog, but he was killed on the farm by machinery. We had numerous farm dogs that were just pets or a complete nuisance. Some saw their mission in life as chasing cars and barking at tyres. They either refused to accompany us for the cows or made them walk too fast, usually when the weather was wet and the ground soft, thereby causing damage. My father always used the excuse that we, the children, had spoiled the dogs, as they preferred to stay with us than go with him to work. I suspect his lack of patience also had something to do with it!

One of the more memorable dogs was Floss, as she had pups once at the beginning of our summer holidays. She created a nest for herself in a hole under the trunk of a tree so we had to move them all to the hayshed. Once they were old enough to move around, we played with them constantly for the entire summer. They were put into prams and wheeled about. They were brought for rides in the front baskets of our bikes and carried in our arms to see if they would show any inclination for rounding up cows. We found good homes for four of the five pups and kept one ourselves.

The one disadvantage of dogs for farmers, particularly sheep farmers, is the potential damage they can do to a flock of sheep. When dogs get together with others, the instinct to hunt can take over – and this applies to all dogs, no matter how much of a gentle pet they appear to be. One day, a year or so after Brian and I had moved back to Ireland, my parents were away and we were looking after the two dogs on the farm. Both were pets, totally useless regarding working cattle but gentle, unassuming, ordinary pet dogs. Brian heard a commotion in a neighbour's field beside High Shores and found both of them attacking a ewe. It was horrible for so many reasons: the guilt that our dogs had done such a thing, the regret that a sheep had been bitten and traumatised, the awkwardness with our neighbours. Understandably, they weren't happy. The dogs weren't put down but we promised that they wouldn't be able to roam freely without supervision in the future.

SAM

When Brian and I came back to Ireland in 2002, we didn't have a dog. Looking back, I don't know how we managed without one, or how, when I was a child, we managed with dogs that were useless in terms of following instructions and being reliable. Many a time we rounded up calves or yearlings to move them to another field or bring them in for dosing. Sometimes it happened that they were all almost at the gate when a few made a break for it and the others then followed suit. Then we'd have to start again. It probably only happened a couple of times but it must have left scars because I remember that frustration, not to mention the panting and puffing, very vividly.

Sam came from sound parentage; they were good working dogs but without any pedigree and it was an unplanned pregnancy. He came to us when he was eight weeks old in October 2007, a time of year when there isn't much happening on the farm as all livestock would be put indoors soon. He showed promise from an early age. We only had him a couple of weeks when he took off in hot pursuit of a batch of weanling calves. The instinct was there and we knew he would be a good one. After we had named him, it seemed like everyone I knew that had a baby boy named their son Sam. I decided I'd never call a dog a human name again, as they might not look upon sharing a name with our dog as a compliment.

Sam spent a lot of time with Brian on the tractor and the two soon become inseparable. A good dog on the tractor makes perfect company, as you can chat or have a very companionable silence. Sam travelled on the loader too, his nose over the half door and looking out to view everything along the road, just as every farmer is interested in whatever is over the hedges. He did all the things that normal pups do; we couldn't leave our wellies outside the back door as he decided they were playthings to throw around.

Today, Sam has two great loves in his life: the loader

and the challenge of working young cattle or bulls. He runs alongside the bucket or bale spike of the loader. He accompanies Brian as he drives up to Kerr's Farm, and as Brian pushes in the bale of silage Sam keeps the cattle back inside the open gate. On one particular day, Brian was on the way up there when he realised Sam hadn't accompanied him. He was cross, but as he got to the sheds, he realised he didn't have the right attachment on the front of the loader. He was doubly irritated now and returned to the yard in a bad mood to see Sam waiting patiently for him beside the bale spike – the implement Brian needed. Yes, Sam knew what the next job of the day was and exactly what was needed for it.

It would be much more difficult to manage bulls without Sam. He is fearless and determined when it comes to loading bulls onto a cattle trailer. We rarely go into the loading pen with the bulls, just stand back and tell Sam to 'bring them on'. He hardly ever barks, but from the age of two he discovered that having a bark was useful with difficult cattle. He was kicked in the head by a bull once and was stumbling around afterwards. We rang the vet and were advised to bring him in. There was a slight delay as he was so filthy from running around in the muck – we had to wash his legs and cut off the worst of the matted long hair before we felt we could bring him into a clean surgery. When we got there, he seemed to remember having been there before, from when he was castrated, and didn't want to go in. It turned out to be concussion and after a couple of days' rest he was fine.

Sam adores Brian. He's hugely loyal, often staying at the back door when Brian is in the house having his dinner or tea. He even occasionally growls at contractors if they try to leave after dinner and Brian is staying inside to do something.

They have to call Brian to tell Sam to let them out. He pines for Brian when we go away on our annual holiday. If Brian goes to the outfarm and doesn't bring him, he comes down to the back door and waits for him to return. If Brian is in another part of the farm and he wants to find him, he'll sniff him out, no matter how far away the field is.

He's mischievous too at times. One day, Brian and Sam were working in Doonane and were going to be late home for dinner. The children had got their school reports and wanted Brian to see them, so we packed up a picnic and went over to eat there. As we were rereading the reports and enjoying a cup of tea, we turned around to find Sam had eaten all the queen cakes.

His only disadvantage, as far as I am concerned, is that he only obeys Brian. He might do what I tell him to do or he might not. If he decides he knows best, he just point blank ignores me. There's many the time I've been rounding up cattle with him and he just did it his way, pointedly ignoring me, as if to say, 'You haven't a clue and I know what I'm doing.' It's true every dog has only one master.

Sam loves a challenge and as he got older he became bored by tame jobs like bringing in the cows with me. Sometimes he comes for them, sometimes he doesn't. As he was starting to slow down we decided to look out for a second dog, as if something happened to Sam we'd never manage without him. A neighbour had advertised pups in the local creamery, so Brian and Kate went to have a look and brought home a four-month-old bitch. Sam didn't know what to make of her at first, as he hadn't seen another dog for years, but within a few days they'd become good friends. Lou has been great for him, as they play rough and tumble together in the summer evenings and it's like he has recaptured his youth. We only realised how elderly he has become when we compared his antics to the lively four-month-old pup. We felt a bit guilty, as we wondered if we had deprived him of fun with other dogs for years.

Sam is semi-retired now, his muzzle is going grey and he chooses his jobs. He's like a supervisor or a retired farmer; in the mornings he strolls around the yard to check everything is as it should be. If he could talk, I'm pretty sure he'd be telling me what to do. He sometimes comes for the cows, but he lets Lou do all the work and wanders around sniffing out interesting smells. He still comes along at the end and insists on claiming credit for a job well done. If it's a long way to the field or the weather isn't pleasant, you can see him thinking, 'Sod the hardship,' and he wanders over to the hayshed to lie down on some loose straw. But if it's a case of working with young stock, particularly young bulls, wild horses wouldn't keep him away and he's still very skilled at loading cattle onto a trailer. Even the driver who brings our cattle to the factory always comments on his skill and says he's the best dog around. He keeps any foxes at bay, too, by patrolling the garden boundary and barking profusely to warn them off.

Sam is usually put back into his kennel while the cows are being milked because he used to get a bit carried away in his minding of them in the collecting yard. If he gets to stay out, he is overjoyed. One winter morning when Brian was letting cows out of the new cubicle shed, one took a notion to head off in the opposite direction for a wander and the others followed. Of course, it would be the morning the wire wasn't across to stop them going any further, so they kept walking.

Brian had to get Sam to get them back and, as a reward, let him stay out. When I came out to the yard half an hour later, I met a dog grinning from ear to ear. He was so delighted with himself that he reminded me of a child being allowed up past their bedtime. This was made even better by the fact that Lou was still in her kennel. Occasionally Brian lets him stay out as a treat when he is milking, and he knows to be on his best behaviour. Sometimes he will forget himself and give a little bark in his excitement, but when Brian yells at him to be quiet, he'll give an apologetic wag of the tail as if to say, 'I know I'm not supposed to be here but I promise I'll be good.' It's amazing how much can be communicated by the angle of a dog's head and the exuberance of his tail wag.

LUTHIEN AMÁRACH – A WORKING DOG

It's been years since I've had a dog of my own, and I've never had a working dog who obeyed me. But now we have Lou. Her full name is Luthien Amárach. 'Luthien' is inspired by a Tolkien novel and 'Amárach' is Gaelic for 'tomorrow' or 'of the future'. It's abbreviated to Lou. She was everyone's dog at first. Overjoyed to see any of us in the mornings, she always comes running when we call her. She's half the size of Sam, and for the first couple of weeks when we called her we couldn't see her in our eyeline. We'd be looking around the yard and, after a minute or two, would look down and discover she was at our feet looking up as if to say, 'I'm here.'

She's great at bringing in the cows, she's good at rounding up cattle, and when taking cattle out of a shed or field, she never leaves one behind, whereas Sam had got complacent and just presumed the last ones would follow him.

Like all beings, Lou's not perfect and has a few flaws. She's not overly keen on being on the loader or tractor. Although she can jump up high, she refuses to jump up onto them. I think this is because we often lift Sam up, as he struggles with the jump in his old age, so she thinks she should be lifted up too. She is useless at loading cattle into a trailer – she goes under the trailer ramp and yaps. She is clueless with vehicles, as she tends to go under them when they're stationary, so we have to keep a good eye on her.

She doesn't have a good sense of direction or smell. Sam will find Brian wherever he is on the farm, even if he's in the furthest field, whereas if I go somewhere and Lou doesn't notice, she then traverses all over the place looking for me. They say dogs can be like their owners, and I guess she and I share the same terrible sense of direction.

If Brian lets her out of the shed and she knows I'm somewhere around the yard, she'll race across to me. She follows my instructions, responding immediately. She obeys Brian only if I'm not around. She waits until I give her the signal to round up the cattle or cows – it is so nice knowing she will wait until I give her the instruction. Brian has been caught out once or twice when he's put a gate across the yard – which signals he's going to get the cows – but then he's been distracted by something and forgotten to tell her to 'wait'. By the time he's realised Lou has gone, she's in the field and has the cows rounded up. She doesn't bark at them yet (Sam was two years old before he did), so if a cow is in a world of her own and doesn't realise Lou is there, it can be quite funny; Lou looks at me as if to say, 'What else am I supposed to do?'

One day we were in the outfarm and gave her a command to get the calves from the top of the field. She went off like a bullet. Brian was sorting out the gates and I went walking after her with Sam beside me. I was wondering why the calves weren't being rounded up and when I got there, there was no sign of her. I called her and rang Brian to see if she'd returned to him. He remembered she'd helped him the previous day with the cattle across the road – maybe she had thought she was to round *them* up? My heart was in my mouth for a minute, as she would have crossed the road. We went across and, yes, she had all those cattle in a corner. Her error was down to our poor communication or perhaps her bad sense of direction.

When I'm working in any of the sheds scraping cubicles or feeding calves, she noses around entertaining herself but comes over to me every now and then to check I'm still there and to let me know she's around. This reminds me of when the children were small and, when at a toddler group or a party, every now and then they'd come over to me as if to reassure themselves I was there and go off again happy. And just as we had to spell words occasionally in front of the children, we have to spell 'C-O-W-S' in front of Lou too.

Although she likes stalking the farm cats and I've seen her chase birds occasionally, it never occurred to me to warn her off touching the hens, as Sam had never gone near them. The three hens were in semi-retirement – I was getting about one egg every three or four days from them – and I was going to let them enjoy their old age. They roamed everywhere and always came back in the evenings.

Then, one evening, one hen didn't turn up and I went looking for her. I found her in the hayshed, dead, and with no apparent injuries apart from a single puncture wound near her neck. I presumed it was a mink and was planning on getting a mink cage and whatever else I might need. I was keeping the two remaining hens indoors for most of the day, just letting them out in the evening for an hour when there was someone in the yard making a noise. Then one evening I let them out at 5 p.m.; Brian was coming in for dinner and the dogs were around. Brian rang me around 6.15 p.m., saying he'd found the two hens dead in the hayshed. The dogs usually stay around the back door when we are inside, but that evening I had to call Lou a few times before she arrived for her dinner. Had she killed the poor hens? The jury was out, but I wasn't taking any chances and, as yet, I haven't got around to replacing them. When I do, I'll have to keep a close eye on her and be ready to warn her off the second she goes near them.

I recently moved calves from one field to another in the outfarm. Brian suggested I bring both dogs with me, as it was going to be awkward. It is a large field and the gateway is midway along the hedgerow. I brought Lou and we were both chuffed with our success. She brought the weanlings up along by the ditch slowly and steadily, while I directed them through the gateway. A couple evaded me but she sped past to get them back. Watching a good dog working cattle or sheep is like watching poetry in motion – their skill, their speed, their joy – and even though they enjoy receiving praise when the task is finished, they get most delight from the journey, not the achievement of the goal.

Lou will stop doing absolutely anything else, even stalking a cat, if she hears the words 'cow' or 'come on, ladies'. Even though she prefers being with me, if she hears Brian call her to help move cattle from a shed, she is off like a bullet towards him. We couldn't ask for a more enthusiastic dog.

What makes Lou a special dog? She's always good-humoured, always glad to see us, always attentive. She doesn't mind whether I chat or whether I'm silent – she signals her acknowledgement of whatever I have said with a wag of her tail or a quizzical raised eyebrow. She's got me out of a pickle when cows were spooked and when I left the wrong gate open and cows went into the wrong field! I don't do anything on the farm now without her being with me. When I'm in the house for part of the day, she's happy lying there watching me typing and occasionally she'll come over to remind me that she's there.

Is she my best friend? Well, she is always pleased to see me, listens if I talk, is quiet if I want silence, obeys me, understands my instructions, is my first port of call if cattle end up where they shouldn't be, hears me when I call her (she never has selective hearing), is very contented, and lies down and gazes at me lovingly for hours. Yes, Lou is definitely my best buddy.

Brian sometimes groans, 'There will never be another dog like Sam.' I feel the same about Lou. It's true that a dog is always a farmer's best friend.

12

THE CALVING SEASON

The future of every dairy and beef farm lies in its calves. Without them, there wouldn't be heifers to go into the milking or suckler herd and there wouldn't be any animals to sell to the factory or mart. In 1930s Ireland, however, farmers were being paid to dispose of calves. The 'economic war' with Britain was in full flow. As the Irish government refused to pay Britain the land annuities, the British government rejected Irish imports. This was a real problem, as two-thirds of Irish beef had been going across the Irish Sea in the early 1930s, and much like the present-day situation Irish farmers were very dependent on the British market. Éamon de Valera, a head of government at the time, was determined that 'Ireland would starve Britain', but in the meantime the value of cattle plummeted from £8–£10 each in the early 1930s to £2–£3 in 1935. Farmers who held onto cattle the previous year hoping the price would increase found that they were almost worthless. Calves worth £2 three years previously had devalued to a couple of shillings.

The government agreed to pay ten shillings for each calfskin, seeing it as a means of drying up Britain's beef supply. Farmers could slaughter their newborn calves and submit the calfskins for payment. In time, farmers came to regret this decision, when it was recognised that the price of beef was improving again – and at a time when many of these calves would have matured. The scheme was over-subscribed, as within its calculations the government hadn't included the twenty-five per cent of calves that died of disease or were stillborn each year. Farmers skinned these and submitted them for payment. As a result, the assessors became stricter about the quality of the calfskins; any nicks in the skin and the farmer didn't receive a payout. It wasn't a good decade in Irish farming. These days there would be a huge outcry from farmers and the general population.

I heard a story of a cow dying close to calving. The farmer got a neighbour to help him do a post-mortem to see if they could establish the cause of death. They found twin bulls nearly to term, so they were skinned and submitted for payment. I suppose there is a silver lining in every situation, but a bleak one at that.

Thankfully, by the 1940s, the value of beef had increased and calves were very much needed alive.

A DIFFICULT CALVING

In Dad's day, if a cow was having trouble calving, neighbours were called upon to help. Ropes were applied above the calf's hooves, the cow was restrained, and strong men pulled as hard as they could to deliver the calf. Thankfully, much more can be done now to ease the delivery. There's more research into the sires, for a start, so farmers know if bulls are proven to be easy calving. If assistance is required, there are now various tools available, which means pressure and pull can be applied and controlled without the need for five men. If a calf is too big to be delivered naturally, then the answer is a caesarean section by a vet, but thankfully they are rare on this farm – two have been performed in the last fifteen years.

Sometimes calves are born coming backwards. The norm is that the front hooves present first, followed by the calf's nose lying along its front legs. A calf coming backwards usually needs assistance. Normally, the nose and head pulsate against the cervix, encouraging gradual opening, whereas the calf's hips don't have the same persuasive effect. It's not overly nice for the cow either, as it's more uncomfortable to deliver with the hips coming first, as it's the biggest area. A further complication is that once the calf is half out and the umbilical cord breaks, the calf could suffocate or suffer brain damage if there's a delay in getting oxygen.

The first sign that a calf is presented backwards is the position of its hooves. Alabaster-white, they show the cleats pointing upwards if the calf is presented normally, but are sometimes downwards if the back legs are coming first. I was commandeered to help when Dad checked a calving cow and found a tail rather than a head. The hooves and hocks were large, so he reckoned it was a big bull calf. We had purchased a ratchet, so this was going to be its first use. Previously, it was a case of tying a farmer's knot in a rope, looping another rope through it, tying it to a secure bar at the other side of the shed or cattle crush for leverage and pulling with all your might. This implement was going to do the hard work.

I was in charge of pulling and pushing the ratchet to and fro until we had a firm tension on the rope. The cow was restrained in the cattle crush so she couldn't move forward or back. She just wanted the calf out of her and gave a bellow. I was nearly in tears for her. She was being so patient and I wondered if she understood we were doing our best to help her. Dad was speaking soothingly to her tail, more so talking to himself than the cow. If the calf got stuck at the shoulders for a few moments, it would be a disaster, as it could smother, so we had to be as sure as possible that the timing was right. As Dad told me to pull and push the ratchet, he was supporting the body of the calf as it emerged. It's important the calf doesn't fall down straight too quickly or its ribs could be damaged, or it could hit its head off the ground. It was a big calf and, as the hips emerged, Dad staggered a little with the weight and laid it down on the straw.

We didn't have time to give a sigh of relief as it didn't seem to be breathing. The first port of call was to tickle its nose with a bit of straw – well, more vigorously than a tickle; I was pushing the straw right up its nostril while Dad was rubbing its sides. After a few seconds, the calf snorted and shook its head. The next thing was to ensure the fluid was drained from its lungs. The fluid comes out gradually during a normal birth with the forward pulsing, but can damage the lungs if left in there. Dad lifted the calf up high by its back legs and hoisted them over the gate to the pen while I held its hooves still. Dad rubbed the calf's sides in a downward motion to encourage release of fluid and the calf shook its head again as fluid came out of its mouth. Poor thing, but it was alive. Once the calf was lowered to the ground again, we checked the sex and, yes, it was a male as suspected. We put him into the wheelbarrow and transported him to one of the stone sheds, then returned to release his mother from the crush so she could join him. Pain forgotten, she was anxious to meet her offspring and immediately proceeded to lick him all over. Having been licked occasionally by a cow when feeding them, I know how vigorous and sandpaper-like their tongues are. He would be warm and dry in no time.

Just twenty minutes after being born, it seemed incredible he had ever been inside her. How had this body and its long sprawling legs managed to fit in there? As it was getting late, Dad decided to leave him for a few minutes to see if he would suckle rather than having to milk the cow and feed the calf. Nowadays we always bottle feed the calf so we know how much colostrum it has drunk. He went to check on another cow due to calve and I leaned over the half door to watch them.

Sometimes it can take a while for a newborn to get to their feet, especially after a difficult birth, but this was a hardy chap. By the time Dad returned about twenty minutes later, he was starting to stagger to his feet, the cow giving him encouraging nudges with her nose. Just as he had all four legs reasonably straight and upright, she nudged him a little too vigorously. He took a nosedive, his back legs remaining straight but his front legs buckled under him. Undeterred he tried again, and again, and nosed his way to her udder. She stood perfectly still, just turning her head as if to say, 'That's it, my boy, it is right there.'

It amazed me then, and it still does today, how quickly newborn calves can get to their feet and find their way to the source of milk. Not all do and that's when human help is required, but the fact so many manage it independently seems nothing short of miraculous.

FEEDING CALVES

In Garrendenny, the calves were housed in a long row of seven or eight terraced stone sheds. Each was separated by walls about four feet high. One summer, my cousin and I spent a pleasurable afternoon racing each other from one end of the calf sheds to the other, climbing over each wall as we went. We were slightly concerned that evening when we were warned we could end up with ringworm all over our bodies, but luckily it never materialised.

There were four calves in each shed and they drank milk from buckets, two heads fitting into each bucket. It wasn't an easy task to open the door and stop them rushing out. The buckets had to be put down without spilling the milk.

Calves' resistance to diseases comes in the form of their dam's colostrum. The newborn calf needs between two and four litres of colostrum – depending on its breed and size – ideally in the first two hours of life, to maximise its chances of excellent health.

Helping to feed calves one evening when I was about nine years old, I was warned not to spill the colostrum as the two buckets were half full of this valuable liquid. It was a freezing cold night with ice on parts of the yard. The slope leading from the milking parlour door was steep and, of course, I stepped on the iciest part. As I felt my feet go up in the air, I slammed the two buckets down so their base hit the ground rather than turning over. This action also protected my coccyx but meant the back of my head hit off the concrete and I saw stars. I lay there for a moment, stunned, but my main concern was for the milk. I still remember the relief that I hadn't spilled any of it.

The calves were fed from buckets for decades and we changed to feeding them from teat feeders only a few years ago. It makes it much easier, especially when training them to drink. Why? Well, it's a calf's instinct to raise its head up to a teat on its mother's udder so trying to persuade it to lower its head into a bucket needed a lot of patience at times.

Dad taught me how to train newborn calves to drink. I put one or two fingers of my left hand into its mouth and, scooping up a little milk with my right palm, poured it into its mouth. Once it got the taste of the milk combined with thinking it had a teat, not a finger, in its mouth, the calf's head lowered to drink the milk in the bucket. Sometimes I could actually see its brain joining the dots and realising what it was supposed to be doing. Once it started to swallow milk, I removed my hand. Sometimes the calf preferred to suck the finger rather than drink the milk, and I've found, to my cost, that if I left my hand there for too long, the calf then expected it to be there at every feed.

Some farmers had no patience for training calves to milk. They pushed the calf's head down into the bucket of milk. The poor helper holding the bucket, usually a child, was shouted at, as the weight also pushed the bucket down towards the ground when it was supposed to be held up. The calf was bound to struggle, as it thought it would drown, and its natural instinct was to pull its mouth and nose out of the milk. No wonder calf-rearing was viewed as women's work – lots of men just didn't have the patience or the understanding.

161

Thankfully it's rare but a calf can be a poor feeder, and while we can now use a stomach tube to get the milk into them if necessary, farmers in the past had to rely on perseverance. One of my aunts apparently threw the remains of the milk over a calf in frustration after struggling to get it to drink and said, 'It can soak in!'

I've never been that bad, but I have had to walk away for a few minutes on occasion when it feels like I'm sweating buckets and the milk is going cold. I calm down and the calf's brain has a chance to register, 'Oh, that stuff was nice and now it's gone. I'd better drink it if it comes back in case it disappears again.' Once a stubborn or reluctant calf starts to drink, a wave of relief washes over me.

Now that we use teat feeders, I train them to suck using a three-litre bottle and quite often they will be on the teat feeder by the second or third feed. Feeding calves is a great job for young children. When small, Will and Kate used to carry milk across in small buckets to the calf shed. It's a huge help having a child bottle feed a calf while I'm training others onto a teat feeder. As feeding a newborn calf can take between six and fifteen minutes, this is a big time-saver when there could be four or five newborns requiring bottles. It makes the children feel useful too. I've noticed they never mind helping if they know their contribution carries value in the form of saving Brian or me time. It's what family farming is all about. And happiness really is when a newborn calf guzzles milk down in a few minutes.

When we were young, we chose our own bull calf each spring. At that time, we sold bull calves in the mart and we'd get the £100 or thereabouts to spend and save. Which calf to choose was always a matter of great debate – should we go for nice markings, or for size, or for one who just looked friendly? I always remained fairly satisfied with my choice, watching him as he grew and filled out. My sister, however, always changed her mind as a smaller, cuter calf was born, and yet another, even though it was pointed out that she'd make more money if she chose bigger calves.

I really like Hereford–Friesian calves. The hybrid vigour is certainly there in force and they tend to hoover up anything edible. When all other calves in their pen have finished, they will suck on each teat in turn to get the very last dregs of milk from the feeder. However, one newborn Hereford-cross calf refused point blank to drink, to the extent that she was gritting her teeth against the teat of the bottle. We tube-fed her two or three times but don't like to tube feed too often in case the throat gets damaged or the calf becomes dependent on it. It's rare we have to continue tube feeding unless the calf is very ill. We can't let hunger be its guide in its early days, as it needs as much of the mother's early milk as possible. I ended up calling her Mary, Mary, Quite Contrary as this three-day-old calf wasn't taking anything for me. Suggestions from farmers on Twitter included sprinkling sugar on her tongue, sprinkling salt on her tongue, putting honey or marmalade on the teat, giving her a square of dark chocolate, or administering vitamin E.

I didn't have any vitamin E so I went out armed with a little container of sugar and a bottle of honey. She's female, so I decided to try the sweet option first. Making her thirsty by giving her salt didn't appeal to me at all. I didn't have dark chocolate but I tucked a bar of caramel chocolate into my pocket just in case.

I put three dessertspoonfuls of sugar on her tongue and she just ground it in her mouth but it didn't make her want the milk. She was still gritting her teeth. I had her pinned in the corner of the pen with her head in a headlock under my arm – I could feel the sweat trickling down my back – and she still refused to drink. I threw my hat out of the pen as I was overheating, grabbed the bottle of honey and poured a huge dollop into the milk. I also drizzled it generously over the teat. This was sink or swim time. If this didn't work, she'd have to wait till the morning for a feed. She sucked and slobbered initially and then, miraculously, she sucked and sucked until it was all gone. The honey had worked. Like many females, she had a sweet tooth – I couldn't criticise her for that. I rewarded myself with the bar of chocolate that evening.

The next morning, once she heard me coming, she was up and looking for milk. She latched onto the feeder in seconds and guzzled it down. She never looked back after that, although she kept the name Contrary Mary.

WHEN CALVES FALL SICK

Calves are susceptible to a number of diseases. The most dreaded was the white scour, a severe form of diarrhoea. Calves can get very dehydrated in a very short time and then death isn't far away. In the 1940s and 1950s, it was believed by some that cow's milk was too rich for scouring calves and they diluted the milk with water. This was a disaster, as the water made it more difficult for them to digest the liquid at a time when their system was under stress. Other cures included half feeds of milk with two spoonfuls of castor oil, twenty drops of laudanum, and half a glass of whisky and wine every day for nine days. A penny's worth of envelopes cut up and boiled in milk was another suggestion. A pint of glucose and water every hour was also advised by some and I'd imagine would have been the most effective cure. Depending on the cause of the scour, it was usually contagious and spread from one calf to another. Younger calves wouldn't have much resilience and may have died within twenty-four hours. Over a quarter of the calves born in a year died from disease or other causes then.

When calves get sick, it can be almost as time-consuming as looking after a sick child, except rather than having one or two children wanting to sit on your knee, there are usually quite a few calves to divide your time between.

A few years ago, a number of our calves got cryptosporidiosis, a very contagious diarrheal disease caused by microscopic parasites. It now reoccurs every year even though we do everything possible to prevent it. Older calves at six weeks old are sturdy and can withstand a bout of diarrhoea and missing a feed, but it can have a serious effect on younger calves. Treatment includes administering electrolytes but if a calf is very ill, sometimes the only recourse is to get the vet to put them on a drip. It is amazing to watch a calf who almost seemed at death's door show signs of recovery within hours.

One evening there were three calves scouring with cryptosporidiosis. We had used a kit to test their faecal samples. We removed them from their pens and put them into an isolation unit with a heat lamp over them. Two of them had been named so I already had a soft spot for them. Red Clover, Lottie and bull calf number 2483 didn't look happy. Number 2483 was a small calf, mostly white, and looking very thin, miserable and sorry for himself. Red Clover's mother is almost totally black, with a white tip on her tail and four white socks. Red Clover has identical white markings but she is completely red; she could almost be mistaken for a Limousin calf. Lottie didn't have any markings of note but Brian informed me she was one of the highest EBI heifers born to date, with the potential to become one of our best cows, so there was no pressure at all regarding keeping her alive and well!

They weren't too bad at 8 p.m., but at 10 p.m. I was getting concerned. As fast as I got liquids into them, it came shooting out the other end. Experts say that two litres of oral electrolytes every four hours is sufficient but I felt that was going to be too long a gap. They didn't want to drink so I had a choice between stomach tubing them or dosing them. They were so poorly I used a 60 ml syringe to get the fluids into them. I gave two litres between the three calves, taking it in turns to give each one five syringefuls at a time.

I went out again at 11.30 p.m. and at 1.30 a.m. At 1.30 a.m. I was regretting not having called the vet. They hadn't moved since the previous feed. I was wondering if they'd be alive in the morning. I dosed them again. They didn't even want to swallow: it was more an involuntary action as I put the 60 ml of liquid down the back of their mouths. They didn't look any livelier after getting approximately 700 ml each. I went inside to lie down on the sofa for an hour, setting alarms on my phone just in case.

When I went out again at 3 a.m., they were looking so much brighter. Lottie was standing up and the others had changed positions. At the 4.30 a.m. feed, two were standing. I went to bed then and Brian did the 6 a.m. feed before he

166

milked. I got up at 8 a.m. to see three calves standing up and looking at me as if to say, 'Where's my milk?' They don't appreciate me one jot for it but I'll always have a soft spot for each of them. Lottie and Red Clover are in the milking herd this year as first-time calvers and I'm looking forward to seeing how they get on. Some experts say scour in a heifer calf affects her lifetime production of milk, but so far we haven't seen any evidence for it, as any cows now milking that contracted cryptosporidium are performing as expected according to their genotyping results.

If you're wondering how we remember all their names, we don't name all of them. It's hard enough to remember tag numbers let alone names, but sometimes a name suits a calf. She or he gets a name and that bit more attention because they are ill, or cheeky, or a poor feeder, or greedy, or quiet, or small but feisty, or big and bolshy.

13

A LITTLE BIT OF LUCK
GOES A LONG WAY

We always seem to be a little bit anxious at the start of the calving season. It's important to get a good start, with some nice strong calves. Occasionally, one or two cows may calve early with a stillborn and this always causes concern that there will be more. We always get any dead calves tested in the vet lab and the results are almost always either inconclusive or 'one of those things'. Even though the cows are vaccinated, it's a worry that the cause could be something infectious that results in abortions, such as salmonella or leptospirosis. If something does go wrong, it's easy to blame ourselves even if nothing could have been done. We tell ourselves that things go wrong in human maternity hospitals too, places where they have monitors and specialists and lots of staff. Thankfully these incidents are few and far between.

Farmers are always grateful for a bit of good luck during calving. That might be arriving in the nick of time after a cow has delivered a calf which is still in its membrane, and being able to save it from smothering by bursting the bag. A few years ago, we had an exceptionally lucky night. It had been a busy week, with twenty-six calves being born in three days. Brian slept through a couple of alarms and arrived out to find a cow had just given birth to a calf coming backwards and all was fine. Another cow was calving and a fine heifer calf was born within minutes. After feeding both with colostrum that was in the fridge, he did a quick check on others and went back to bed. Getting up three hours later, he discovered the recently calved cow had a second calf beside her. It was a heifer and was alive and well. The mother had been pregnant with twins and we hadn't realised. Checking the other maternity pen, a calf had just been born and was still in a membrane. If he hadn't been there, it could have smothered within minutes. Sometimes good things, as well as bad, come in threes.

The birth of twins always makes us smile. If truth be told, twin calves are not always a positive because the mother may take more time to recover or it may take longer for her to go in calf again. As with twin births in humans, complications can arise. A female calf that is twin to a bull is almost certainly infertile. The testosterone in the womb from the male renders the female calf sterile, and she is what's known as a freemartin. In a dairy herd, a single female calf is worth more money than a male and an infertile female.

We had one twin freemartin heifer a couple of years ago that was seen on heat, and she subsequently went in calf and is still in the herd. This may have happened because her reproductive system developed when the levels of testosterone were low. It is rare, though. Apparently bovines are the only animals that this happens with – goats and sheep can birth male and female twins and all will be fertile. It's not all about money, though, and no matter what the sex, there's always a feeling that good luck is smiling on you when twins are born and doing well.

Do twins stay close throughout their lives? Do they know they shared a space in the womb and does that create a bond? We have had twin heifers who maintained close relationships throughout life. One set of twins were separated as yearlings for a while into two different batches and yet, when reunited, continued to always graze close by each other and came into the milking parlour in the same row. I've noticed twin calves always lying close to each other in the pens and they will stand side by side when sucking from the teat feeder even if in a pen of nine calves. It just shows blood is thicker than water, although sometimes two unrelated cows will form a mother–daughter type of bond, where one will be very protective of the other.

About ten years ago a cow had triplets. It's very rare that this happens in cows, about one in 10,000, and it was the first time it had happened on this farm. We had to get the vet to help us deliver them, such was the entwinement of legs. She had two bull calves, and luckily the vet checked her again and found another one in there, a heifer. The same night, as if there wasn't enough drama, one of our goats had quintuplets. One was born fine, and when it became clear that no more were coming, we decided to investigate. I found it quite traumatic, as they were so entangled that she needed help. A goat is so much smaller than a cow when it comes to getting your hand in there! However, all went well and we had five little goat kids the next morning. Eight offspring from two mothers is some night's work. The children enjoyed choosing names for all of them the next morning.

Farmers have to take care of their own safety too. Sometimes the prevention of accidents is down to preparation and common sense, and sometimes it's simply due to good luck. I was probably eleven or twelve, and upon seeing that a calf had just been born, walked over to the feeding barrier to take a closer look and check everything was all right. The mother was busy licking it. Without me realising, the dog was in the feeding passage standing behind me. The first-time mother started to paw the ground and looked as though she was about to headbutt her calf. Fresh in my mind was a recent birth where Dad had to reach in and pull a calf away from its mother. It's rare but it can happen that a first-timer attacks her offspring and could even kill the calf if it isn't removed from her. I thought this was going to be a repeat and I was halfway through the gap in the feeding barrier when I heard Dad shout at me to get out. She wasn't going to attack the calf; she was concerned the dog or I was going to hurt it, and she was warning us off. If I'd gone in, she might have attacked me.

Sometimes a cow doesn't carry her calf to full term. If born very early, they are usually stillborn. Shortly after Brian and I arrived back in Ireland, an Angus–Friesian bull calf was born about six weeks premature, no bigger than a collie dog. He needed smaller-than-normal feeds at regular intervals. He grew to match his comrades in size but he was always a special one. We presume it was because he was handled more and for longer as a young calf, but he always came over to Brian when he was herding them. He'd get a head scratch and then amble off again.

Then it came to them being fattened and taken to the factory. Brian normally doesn't go down to see them in the pens once they have been unloaded, but on this occasion he did. The black Angus was at the far side of the pen, but he moved through the others to come over to Brian for a head scratch. He was calm despite the change in surroundings. Farmers are not allowed to remove an animal from the factory once it has been unloaded, and in any case it wouldn't make economic sense to keep a bullock for years and years, but Brian was sorely tempted to get the tractor and trailer and load him up. Yes, there's often a special one you'll never forget.

14

SUPERSTITIONS: THE LUCK OF THE IRISH

D o we still believe in superstitions and magic? The Irish belief in fairies waned over the years, largely due to the coming of electricity, but there's still a respect for fairy forts and a persistent belief in many superstitions. In the 1950s when electricity was being installed in thousands of rural homes, it was said that workers suffered accidents after disturbing fairy rings to lay cables or erect poles. As recently as 2007, fairies were blamed for fallen electricity poles in Co. Sligo.

If I see a single magpie, I will look for a second one, and if I spill salt, I'll throw a bit over my shoulder, but they are probably the limits to my superstitions – within my consciousness at least. Saying a fallen fork was the sign of a visitor didn't strike me as strange, as there were always people calling. An itchy ear signalling someone was talking about you, well, that could happen any day of the week. It's pretty obvious why no one should walk under a ladder.

But I realised I was superstitious when pregnant with our

first child. Living in England at the time, a friend wanted to bring me shopping for lots of baby clothes and I was horrified. I had ordered a buggy and car seat but I had no intention of collecting them until after the baby was born. I had purchased one pack of nappies, a pack of white Babygros and a few other essentials, but nothing else was coming into the house. The concept of baby-shower parties where mothers-to-be receive lots of gifts is something I could never take part in. It probably sounds bizarre, but there's a dread that having celebrated something, the celebration might curse the occasion ever happening.

Superstitions used to be part and parcel of everyday life. If the milk didn't thicken to butter when churned, it was blamed on a superstition. If someone came into the house or yard while the butter was being churned, they had to take a turn or otherwise the butter would never form. I quite like this belief, as it meant the woman doing the churning got a brief rest and a little help.

One man, fed up with difficulty creating butter from their milk, travelled to the Red Hills, near the Curragh, to consult Moll Anthony, a lucky woman. She told him to put a two-shilling piece into the churn when they next made butter. When the butter was nearly formed, he must heat the coulter – the large blade on the back of a plough – and put it under the churn. She told him the first woman to come into the house asking to borrow something was the woman who had 'taken the butter', that she was the reason they couldn't form butter from their milk. As long as they didn't fulfil her request, all would return to normal. He followed her instructions. When a woman popped in looking for some salt, he had to stop his wife attacking her, such was the strength of their beliefs.

Of course, the unavailability of butter wasn't because of a curse, but thanks to impoverished pastures and poor grazing – there just wasn't enough butterfat in the milk.

It was believed neighbours could take revenge by destroying your crops. If they placed rotten eggs at the end of drills, took your turnip thinnings or removed moss from the four ditches of a field, it would affect your crop for that year.

Other beliefs local to this area included throwing a tooth over your shoulder to preserve the remaining teeth. If a hen laid a tiny egg on occasion – these are called a fortnale – they were put in the straw thatch on the roof to bring good luck. When walking anywhere for the first time, you could make a wish as you were on strange ground.

Halloween was a great time for games such as ducking for money, trying to take a bite out of an apple hung in a doorway and scooping out a turnip, carving a face and putting a candle inside. We also enjoyed the superstitions. One game was getting someone of marriageable age to put three nuts by the fire and if they burst that person would be married before the next Halloween.

One of our favourite superstitions of Halloween was the belief that whoever got the ring in the barm brack would be next to get married. Our workman was single and we often teased him about a girlfriend. We even sent him a Valentine's card once, pretending it was from a lady called Angela. As Tommy had his tea earlier than us, the table was set for him individually. We used to watch Mum cutting the slices of fruit brack; we examined each slice to see if we could see the ring within and if it wasn't found in the first few slices, we made her keep cutting until she found it. We ensured one of the slices put on his plate contained the ring. One year, Mum was worried in case he had swallowed it, as he never said a word and yet all the brack was gone, but maybe he just got a bit tired of that joke!

15

THE TROUBLE WITH SHEEP ... AND GOATS AND HENS

When we started farming in 2002, there were just bovines on the farm. As a child, I'd have loved some smaller animals. Calves grow so quickly; they are cute for a few days but unless they are handled regularly in preparation for a show or become a pet, they get too big to be considered cute and manageable by a seven-year-old child. I wanted lambs, then piglets, then hens. We did get a dozen or so hens and had them for a few years.

I wanted the children to have some fun with smaller animals but they had to be purposeful. I didn't want to have pets just for the sake of it – even the farm cats have to earn their keep. We supplement their diet of rodents with dried cat food, but they are expected to provide for themselves to an extent and help us out by keeping mice numbers down.

There were goats on the farm years ago. Well, just a single goat, one that was used to the elements, and it ran with the cattle. It was believed a goat prevented the herd getting tuberculosis and prevented abortions in cows. I'd imagine the superstition was also handy in finding a purpose for surplus billy goats. When I was sixteen, we discovered my allergies included cow's milk. Purchasing frozen goat's milk one day, I asked if they could source goat's cheese. I then overheard one woman say to the other with a laugh, 'Goat's cheese, what next?' It's hard to believe now that it was viewed as an exotic product in 1985. In 2005, as the children were also allergic to dairy products for a while, I had an open mind regarding producing goat's milk and cheese but thought I'd better check if I got on well with goats first.

We bought two goats. Megan was a brown Nubian, a yearling, quiet and charming. Becky was in milk and her previous owner said she would continue to milk for another eighteen months without needing to go in kid. She was half British Saaen, half Nubian. Quite tall, grey in colour, with a tendency to put on weight easily, she had a bottom lip that jutted out and a long beard. She wasn't a beauty, and certainly seemed like a dominant, grumpy old woman. We only realised how strong a personality she had as time went on and we compared her to every other goat we had.

Milking goats is quite different to milking cows. You just squeeze goat teats lightly, but with Becky I felt like I was squeezing not skin but dense, tough rubber. She didn't like standing still either, but we persevered. We tolerated each other. I had a little platform for Becky to stand on while she was being milked, with a bucket at the front so she could eat quietly while I milked her. She still didn't like being milked, preferring to fidget. We didn't realise how tough she was to milk until Megan had her first kids and her milk just flowed in comparison. I ended up milking Becky in the milking parlour with the milking machine. Before Brian milked the cows, I got the parlour ready and got Becky in, tying her to the gate. I put a cup lid on two of the clusters and the system worked well.

Brian used to say we were too alike, both of us stubborn, determined females who don't like to see anyone get the better of us. I refused to give in because, well, she was a goat and I was supposed to be the owner and the boss.

Goats don't like wind and rain. We might think of goats as being happy in all weathers, but they can get ill with pneumonia if left out in the elements. Initially, they were in a fenced part of the garden with an old kennel as a house. It was big enough for them both to stand or lie inside and look out. Then one day it was lashing rain and I looked out the kitchen window to see Becky standing in the doorway, blocking it so Megan couldn't get in. Becky was smirking while poor Megan was standing out in the rain, looking resigned. I had to run out to resolve the situation!

We built them a three-sided shelter in a corner of the field using pallets on three sides and as a roof. Every day, unless it was lashing rain in the morning, they went down to graze and every evening they went back to their shed. At first they were obedient and, although they liked routine, Becky decided she was a bit tired of grass and wherever she went Megan followed. She found the route to the front garden and to the flowerbeds – they were obviously tasty. She ate my expensive potted Japanese Maple, which eventually killed it. On more than one occasion I heard a beep of a car horn from the front of the house and discovered that Becky was standing in the porch, frightening the visitors who had just arrived and were nervous of getting out of the car and ringing the doorbell. She didn't like obeying me when I told her what to do, especially if I took her by the collar to make her march alongside me. I was really impressed with Kate one day when she marched up to Becky, grabbed her by the collar and told her to follow. She did – and as meekly as a lamb.

One day, Becky refused to go to the field and I was getting irritated with her. Megan and her daughter Polly went in happily so I fastened the gate behind them. Becky ran back up the yard, so I shut her into the outer part of the shed. I was feeling smug – let hunger teach her a lesson. That evening, I brought Megan and Polly up from the field to put all three into their shed and I thought Becky looked way too happy for a goat who had spent her day with just a bit of hay to eat. She was grinning from ear to ear. Later, I was telling Brian about Becky's behaviour and he remembered he had bought a bag of ration to try it and had left it in that shed, having only removed a couple of scoops from it that morning. It was incredibly sweet, as it had a high content of molasses. Becky had, until this point, been on a very plain diet, but this was like suddenly getting chocolate cake, profiteroles and caramel ice cream! No wonder she was gloating. We were lucky she hadn't overeaten and become ill.

It was hard to get Becky in kid. I think she was just too tubby for her own good. The signals for being on heat were bleating and twitching, but it was hard to pick up the signs as she was quite vociferous and bolshy anyway. She always went on heat during the busiest of evenings, so it was a rush to get her loaded into the boot of the farm car and bring her to a billy goat. It only suited the owner of the male goats to have Becky served in the evenings, so it was usually 9 p.m. on a cold night, holding her by the lead while waiting for the billy goat to decide if she was attractive or not. Occasionally another billy was brought out if the first wasn't receptive. She spent a whole weekend there once and eventually it worked. Megan, on the other hand, went in kid first time.

Becky had a single kid and Megan had triplets. Becky mellowed considerably with the birth of little Herbie – she absolutely adored him. The difference in her temperament when she had a kid to fuss over was incredible. She was docile, fairly obedient and much less domineering.

Megan was always a complete poppet. She loved routine. She came out of the shed to be milked when I called her, stood quietly, and when finished was happy to go back to the others until I let them out to the field. If something happened to upset the milking routine, such as me answering my phone or forgetting something and going to get it, she followed me and stood there bleating into my ear until I took the hint and milked her. Becky would have used the opportunity to high tail it out of there and go in search of the sweetest leaves in the garden or some ration. Megan and Becky were like chalk and cheese.

After about six years, we sold the goats. It was lovely having them but the paperwork and regulations were becoming tiresome. Keeping a goat register and tagging the kid goats was fine, although extra work at a busy time of year. I recently heard of a farmer who had two pet sheep and was fined five per cent of his Basic Payment Scheme (BPS) imbursement after it was discovered he hadn't kept a sheep register. He hadn't realised he was supposed to do so.

Five adult goats equalled one cow in terms of nitrates and we were pushed to our limit on nitrates. At this stage we had three adult goats and three kids. It was a nuisance transporting them to the billy goat. We didn't have a jeep or a farm car any more, and as the car was fairly new I wasn't overly keen on transporting goats in the boot. While our butcher slaughtered the male goats for us initially, he discovered he had to apply for a specific goat licence, which was going to take time. The only other goat abattoir was fifty miles away.

The children had grown out of their allergies so I was the only one who needed goat's milk. It was a lot of work for milk for my cornflakes and I hadn't metamorphosed into a domestic goddess who created goat's butter, cheese or other products, so in the end the goats were sold to a farmer in Wexford.

We had three pet lambs, too, when the children were small. The farmer who sold them to us was a real gentleman. All three were from triplet births. As the mothers could rear only two, one from each crop was destined to be a 'pet lamb', to be bottle-fed. He ensured all three had been fed colostrum for the first couple of days, and they'd been vaccinated and were fairly strong at three days old. As I had been told sheep like to make a habit of dying, I bought one for each of the children and had a spare! They were fed on milk replacer for a few months and they co-existed reasonably happily with the goats, sharing the shed and the field, although they definitely knew they were different species – they tolerated each other but had no intention of becoming best buddies. Henry and Gordon were destined for the freezer but one day at dinner we were debating whether to keep Matilda or not. Kate, who loved meat even at four years of age, said, 'Oh, no, I can't wait till Matilda is yummy in my tummy.'

Poor Gordon got sick and died. He seemed to be getting better and maybe I took my eye off the ball because when he deteriorated again he went downhill very quickly. I met Dad in the yard and told him Gordon had died. He got a shock, as he thought I was referring to a cousin of his who hadn't been well. Giving animals human names isn't always a good idea! Henry went to the butcher and into the freezer, but Matilda went for a little holiday and came home pregnant.

Some months later, Matilda was sharing a shed with the goats. We didn't want to leave her on her own in case she got lonely and she seemed friendly with Megan and Polly. Megan and Matilda were heavily pregnant and as Megan's udder had become very full, I suspected she was due to kid within days, so I was checking her one night at 3 a.m. When I opened the door, I noticed all three goats were huddled into one corner looking aghast and staring in shock at something on the other side. They couldn't have wormed themselves any further away. Matilda was at the other side of the shed. She had just given birth to a single lamb. The goats' expressions were almost comical, as if to say, 'Where on earth did that come from and what is it?' Poor Matilda looked a bit bewildered too. I went in to get Brian, as I knew very little about sheep and wanted to get her checked in case she was carrying more.

She didn't have any more lambs, just the single ram, which was a good size. The goats were clearly spooked, so we moved Matilda and her lamb to another shed. She seemed more relaxed there and set to licking him again immediately. Within ten minutes, he was standing on shaky little legs and nosing around looking for the udder. Once again it amazed me how a first-time mum who had never seen another sheep give birth knew exactly what to do, as she stood there completely still, just turning her head to look at him and check he was okay.

He was named Harry and, as a male, he went to the butcher too – in the boot of the car. Did we feel sad saying goodbye to him? It may sound cruel, but not really. When you know that's going to be their fate, you accept it – plus, he had a lovely life. He weaned naturally, he had the sweetest of grasses to eat as they roamed the whole farm, he had the sole attention of an adoring mother, and if truth be told he grew into a strong sheep very capable of delivering a strong headbutt to any human if he was so inclined. His cuteness had long disappeared.

Matilda went off on another brief holiday and this time she wasn't so settled when she came back. Maybe she'd had enough of the goats' company, but any chance she got she managed to escape from their paddock and go rambling. She used to stand at the hedge of one of our fields staring across at sheep in our neighbour's fields. When it came close to her time to lamb, we put her on her own to give her space. Once again, it was a 3 a.m. birth. She managed it all on her own. I arrived to find three lambs on the ground beside her and she was busy licking them. Two, a male and a female, were of a good size and there was a tiny female too. Was she big enough to survive, I wondered? Would she have to become a pet lamb? I waited to ensure that they all suckled and then went back to bed.

There was huge excitement the next morning. Once again, the children had a lamb each – and there was a spare! They were named Bill, Sally and Little Lucy. We were wondering about bottle feeding Lucy but a neighbour advised, if the ewe didn't have enough milk, to bottle feed one of the bigger ones, who could then suck a bit but let the smallest one have the mother's milk if at all possible. We kept an eye on them and she seemed to be producing enough milk for all three. They took turns to suckle, so all was well. Lucy was very deft at getting in there and suckled little and often.

Although Matilda seemed more settled for a time, once the neighbour's sheep were in a nearby field again, she was clearly pining for some female adult company. Although she loved her offspring, she wanted to have a good chinwag with other ewes. It was clear the goats were useless for gossip.

Bill went to the factory and then into our freezer and we were wondering what to do with Matilda and her daughters. I didn't want to send either of the girls to the factory. But did we want three breeding ewes? The novelty of the sheep had worn off for the children at this stage, though they were still fond of them.

We sold all three to a neighbour and we were able to see them in their field as we drove by. Matilda had a set of triplets each year, rearing each set on her own. Each year, we'd get a text when she had lambed and we'd pop down to have a look and wish her well with her new offspring.

We also got hens. After all, no farm woman would be viewed as a proper farmer's wife unless she had hens.

I was going to buy a dozen from a poultry farmer who was getting out of egg production. He persuaded me to take another half dozen and, at only €2 each, it was impossible to refuse. They were laying well when we got them so we were getting about sixteen eggs a day.

We made a lot of omelettes and pavlovas, and supplied family and some elderly neighbours with eggs. Many of them lived for another three years, and all but two died of old age.

One got ill and died, and we think the fox got the other one.

Since then, I've had four hens at a time, which is perfect for the amount of eggs we need. They roam everywhere and the fox seems to stay at bay, thanks to Sam the dog. Most have died of old age about six months after they stopped laying. I know if I was a proper farmer's wife I'd wring their necks and prepare them for the pot but we're not that hard up for a chicken dinner and I like to let them live out their retirement.

I got eighteen broilers during the summer a few years ago. They were a day old when purchased and it seemed incredible that something so small could be big enough to provide a dinner in just eight weeks. I was getting fed up seeing whole chickens being sold so cheaply. It seems wrong that an animal had been devalued to such a cheap price, and it also encourages people to presume that a chicken, the main part of a roast dinner, should be cheaper than a coffee and cake. It cost an average of €10 each to rear our chickens. Admittedly they were a lot bigger than the €3 chickens in the supermarkets.

These chickens had a great time roaming around a big shed. We were getting sightings of foxes, so I didn't let them out to roam around the yard. We slaughtered three or four at a time. Brian did the dastardly deed, I plucked them and Brian cleaned them out. By the time we got to the last ones, they must have been five months old and were huge. We had one for Christmas dinner instead of having a turkey.

It was very close to Christmas when the last two were slaughtered. I was busy, so Brian plucked them and then cleaned them out on the scullery table, hanging them up before he went to bed. He hadn't done a thorough job on the plucking but it was late and he decided I could finish them the next day.

In the morning, while the children were having their breakfast, I was making their school lunches and went out to the back hall to get a few sticks for the stove. I let out a screech. There, hanging in my back hall, was a murdered Father Christmas – at least that's what I thought it was for a split second. One chicken had been left hanging high up by the legs so it was 'standing' at my eye level. There were white feathers around the neck and the wings, which resembled Father Christmas's white beard. A slight tear in the skin of the chicken looked like the face had been slashed with a knife. I really wasn't the better of the shock for a few minutes, thinking I'd come face-to-face with a murdered man.

It is lovely to produce your own food, whether it is vegetables from the garden, milk from the cows, eggs from hens or meat from the livestock. I really enjoyed seeing the children interact with and care for smaller animals too, and we ensured they had a good life while they were with us. It's a shame, really, that farming is so busy at certain times of the year that having something extra, such as a pet sheep lambing, is just too much. It's also a shame that the strict regulations can be off-putting, as a mistake with the paperwork could be very expensive. Maybe we're getting old or maybe life is getting busier, but the fun goes out of mixed farming when it adds to the 'chasing your tail all the time' feeling.

16

A FARM CHILDHOOD

TOWN VERSUS COUNTRY

Is life as a farm child so different to that of any other child? I wasn't aware of differences growing up, as the majority of children in my primary school were from farms or lived in rural locations. Even my townie cousins had knowledge of what it was like to live on a farm. In secondary school, most of my friends were from agricultural backgrounds so we spoke the same language. We all knew what drying off cows meant, that the lambing and calving season was a sleep-deprived time of year, that silage cutting meant days of cooking for the women in the house. For me, getting collected by tractor from primary school during snow wasn't such a big deal, whereas for Will and Kate it was hugely exciting, as very few children were being collected with that mode of transport. They understand the relevance of maths homework, as they get the jobs of putting the animal passports in numerical order and they see me working out calculations for mixing milk powder. While some friends had pet rabbits, guinea pigs and hamsters, they had lambs and goat kids. Most of the children's friends in secondary school live in towns and their lives have interesting and sometimes comical contrasts.

JOBS FOR CHILDREN

Non-farming children will help out in the house, paint garden walls, wash the car, cut the grass and probably get a job in a shop or restaurant when in their mid-teens.

Farm kids usually have dedicated chores that need to be done daily. When Will and Kate were twelve and ten, their winter evening chore was to scrape and lime the cow cubicles. They called themselves the James Muck Cleaning Company and presented us with an invoice at the end of each month. Everyone mucks in to help out on a family farm. When a teacher training day is announced, Will knows he won't be spending the day on his Playstation but helping Brian, who is always delighted with the extra pair of hands for tasks like cleaning out a shed or helping with dosing. We like to get some jobs out of the way before Christmas so that we can have some time to relax over the festive few days. The children finished at midday on the last day of term and they came out to help with chores. Kate helped Brian to dry off the cows, Will cleaned out a shed, I scraped and limed cubicles and brought in enough sticks for the fire to last the week.

The differences in language and knowledge between town and farming lives was highlighted to me recently when a parent of one of Will's classmates contacted me to ask if Will would like to go to their house for an afternoon during half-term. I apologised and said he and Brian were doing two days of fencing. She asked if her son could join in. It was then I realised she thought I meant the sport. However, rather than a foil and sabre, Brian and Will were going to be using a post driver, wooden stakes, wire and hammers. I reckoned Brian would have enough on his plate trying to get one teenager to concentrate on keeping stakes in a straight line, so I didn't suggest her son come along.

SMELLS OF A FARM CHILDHOOD

All of us have particular sounds, tastes and smells that call out to us and awaken some memory from childhood. Sometimes they are pleasant and may even suggest an idyllic childhood, sometimes not so much.

Whenever we were irritated by loose wobbly baby teeth, Dad used to tell us how he and his siblings got rid of them when they became loose. One alleged option was to tie a piece of string around the offending tooth, with the other end of the string either tied to your toe or the door handle, and once you moved in the night, the tooth would be yanked out. We decided to let ours wiggle in our mouths until they worked themselves out.

The other method was his father putting his finger and thumb into their mouths to pull it out. As he was a heavy smoker, the smell of tobacco from his hands used to almost make their eyes water as it filled their nose and mouth. People used to say you could sit beside him and not realise he was smoking. He was never seen to exhale. He seemed to inhale the smoke down to his boots – so far down that it never came up again. Every time Dad smelt the smoke of Woodbine cigarettes, he was transported back to having a loose tooth pulled out.

I think, for all farm children, the smell of freshly cut

grass reminds them of mowing grass for hay or silage. And with that smell lies the promise, hopefully, of good banter, picnics in the field, bottles of lemonade, rides on the tractor, sunkissed skin, and long summer days that go on forever, when you don't know what day of the week it is and you don't care.

For Will, grassy smells will bring memories of rides on the contractors' tractors. First the mowing and then the drawing in of the silage, doing his best to escape me when I used to go looking for him at bedtime. He'll remember Brian sending me on a wild goose chase so that he got to go for another two loads, and coming in delighted with himself. He even got a day off school for the silage during his last year in primary school on the pretext that he was helping to cover the pit.

Like all farm children he had an impressive line-up of farm machinery. When the grass was cut in the garden, he used to arrange the cuttings into mini swathes. He drove along with his ride-on tractor and trailer to pick up the grass, putting it in by hand, and then drove to a 'pit' in the bottom of the garden where it was unloaded and rolled with another tractor.

Being so familiar with various smells, we scarcely notice some of them. While we might wrinkle our noses at the whiff of agitated (mixed) slurry or acrid effluent from the silage pit, we may not even notice the pungent smell from fermented silage or odours from the slurry tanks when up the yard. I don't notice a smell from the dogs when outside with them but if Lou sneaks into the kitchen I often get a whiff of damp dog immediately. My parents played a lot of badminton and during the winter season often had a match and a practice once a week. Dad used to race in from milking, eat his tea and then rush upstairs for a shower. We were usually sitting on the sofa reading or watching TV, or we were on the floor playing with Lego. Before he'd grab his badminton racket to leave, we'd get a kiss goodnight. The smell of soap and Old Spice aftershave brings me right back every time. The smell of freshly chopped logs always reminds me of when we had a small room beside the garage, called the 'stick house'. Chopped logs were brought around in the trailer and the room was filled with sticks for the winter. Dad always chopped sticks up quite small. His school teacher only ever asked him to chop sticks once, as he cut them so small they gave out great heat but burned much too quickly.

One day when driving the car, Brian beside me and the children in the back, I was musing that they won't have memories of the smells of our aftershave and perfume conjuring up particular thoughts as we don't go out much. Neither of us are sporty and if we go out socially in the evening once a month, it's probably the maximum.

'We do have smell memories,' said Will from the back of the car.

'You do?' I said, getting excited but puzzled. 'What are they?'

'Sour milk,' was my son's rather dour reply.

It was true. When feeding calves, milk tends to spill on my waterproof trousers, on the front of my coat, on my sleeves, and while I wash the fleecy jackets every few days, I should probably change them daily. Rushing down to get the children from the school bus, the smell used to intensify in the heat of the car.

Then there was the time I had to collect Will at 8 p.m.

after a rugby match. I knew I was running late and although I removed my waterproof trousers and changed my wellies for old trainers, I didn't bother to change anything else. Halfway there, I could smell calves – and it's a bad sign when you can smell it on yourself. A heady mixture of a bit of muck and lots of milk. I told myself it would be okay, I was running late, the other parents would have left and I wouldn't have to get out of the car, so no one would see or smell me. I got there as the bus pulled up in front of me and I knew it would be a few minutes by the time he went to his locker and got back to the school car park. I could see other parents standing out chatting but I resolved to be unsociable and stay in the car.

Then I saw another mother walking over towards me. I consoled myself she was a farmer too, albeit a tillage farmer. As I wound down the window to say hello, the scent of fabric conditioner didn't just waft into the car, it seemed to blast in and circle around my head. All I could do was hope the smell of sour milk dissipated into the fresh air around her as she stood outside. Did I imagine it or did she take a step backwards?

So, my kids, whenever they smell sour milk, will remember their mum! Not quite the memories I wanted to create, but hey ho.

SOUNDS OF FARMING

When I hear the rugby commentary on a Saturday afternoon, I'm transported back to the Saturdays of my childhood. Dad took the afternoon off farming during the Six Nations tournament and watched rugby in the living room while I curled up on an armchair reading one of my Enid Blyton books. The drone of the Kenwood came from the kitchen as Mum made a variety of cakes, often for visitors coming the next day. Every now and then he'd shout for her to come in to watch a replay of a try or a foul. Although I'm pretty sure her interest was negligible, she dropped whatever she was doing and ran in to watch, agreeing it was impressive or terrible. Dad just assumed she was almost as interested as he was. As the smell of baking crept into the living room, I'd leave my comfortable armchair and venture to the kitchen for a queen cake hot from the oven, or even nicer, the cut-off edges from a freshly baked Swiss roll, dusted in caster sugar.

Some things continue, although the people change. Brian doesn't take a Saturday afternoon off to watch sport, although he's happy to watch the highlights, with Will giving a running commentary. Will watches rugby on Saturday afternoons so I still hear the commentary in the background. Instead of Mum using the Kenwood in the kitchen, it's Kate. From the age of nine, she used to suddenly get bored and say, 'I think I'll bake a cake, is that okay?' At first, I used to be nervous of her working with the hot oven and irritated her by hovering around, insisting on taking her baking from the oven, but she soon showed she was more than capable.

Other sounds are the cacophony of calves bawling once the shed door is opened and they are all waiting for their milk. As we are a spring calving herd, it's an annual noise here. Living in the countryside means that there's silence a lot of the time, but that is interrupted by various noises: the distant humming of farm machinery on a balmy summer's evening, the drone of the milking parlour and sometimes the buzz of a chainsaw on a fine autumn's day as farmers cut up a fallen tree for their winter fuel.

One of the most distinctive sounds, from the end of April, of all is the cuckoo. I always struggled to recognise why it was viewed as such a wonderful sound, as it laid eggs in other birds' nests and its offspring were so greedy. Of course, it signals sunshine and the coming of summer – just as much as the sightings of swallows do.

TASTES OF FARMING

Picking blackberries was always a highlight and, just as Mum used to bring us, I brought the children blackberry picking with their seaside buckets, tipping some of my pickings into their little buckets to stop them becoming demoralised. Blackberry and apple tarts and crumbles would be made, and blackberries placed in containers and stored in the freezer.

We also forage for elderflower every year to make cordial and the scent that fills the kitchen spells out summer. Picking wild mushrooms was more satisfying for the children, as those buckets filled up quickly. We don't find mushrooms every year, as they need moisture as well as sunshine in August, but when we do, we celebrate by having them for supper and breakfast. They are cooked in butter and served with buttered white bread and a little bit of salt. Dad always had two fried eggs with his mushrooms.

Baking was a big part of my childhood – not that I did much of it but there was always something homebaked in a tin. Our kitchen was filled with the smells of baking on an almost daily basis: spotted dick, scones, queen cakes, apple tarts, Swiss rolls, coffee cakes and Victorian sponges were the most popular. If there was a death in the vicinity, women brought homemade traybakes to the wake. Fundraisers for parishes or schools always meant another baking bonanza.

I could make fairly decent queen cakes and muffins, but that was about the limit of my culinary skills. We were only back in Ireland a few months when I was invited to contribute to a local fundraiser by bringing home baking and helping out with selling the baked items. A challenge indeed – I knew that if I priced them too high and they didn't sell, that wouldn't go down well with the organisers. If I priced them too low, the bakers wouldn't be impressed. Luckily, an older and more experienced woman was with me and I bowed to her superior knowledge. I spent all day baking to bring plain and decorated queen cakes, four biscuit cakes and two tarts and was very proud of my efforts until I saw the works of art being carried in by others. One lady arrived with her trays of cakes and tarts and they were sold before they even touched the table, such was her wonderful reputation. I had a long way to go – and I haven't got there yet.

A few years ago, I was invited by a magazine to go along to a 'bloggers picnic' for a photoshoot and bring some home baking – what I made was up to me but it had to be 'country style'.

Should I bring brown bread? Scones? Were they too ordinary? I asked another blogger what she was bringing. A sumptuous cake.

Eeek, I thought, is that what was expected? I had been thinking of something more ordinary, not to mention something that could be easily transported.

The researcher phoned me a few days later. On hearing my plans for brown bread and scones, she told me the other blogger was bringing those with some homemade butter, and could I think of something else? I guessed the sumptuous cake had been scrapped.

What could I make? Then I remembered seeing a TV show about the making of clotted cream in Edwardian times. Could I, with my limited resources and limited culinary skills, make clotted cream? I'd be making a product from our own farm – what could be more ideal, if it worked out?

I made three batches and brought the best one. And, amazingly, my clotted cream stole the show! It was gorgeous with the spotted dick and homemade raspberry jam. I had a bottle of elderflower cordial in the freezer from the previous summer, so I put it into a pretty bottle and brought it along. I felt very accomplished in my 'food blogger/perfect farm woman' role, making a gorgeous product from our own milk.

Harvest Thanksgivings are an important date in the farming calendar. It's my favourite service of the year, when the hymns are rousing and cheerful, the church is decorated with flowers, vegetables, fruit and toy farm machinery, and there's often a harvest tea afterwards. A shop-bought contribution just doesn't happen. Rural women are expected to bake, to rattle up something and make it look effortless. Many of them manage it, so the rest of us struggle along and make the best of it, always on the lookout for a recipe that is easy, impresses and doesn't take too much time.

I don't have a light hand when it comes to baking. Kate has inherited my mum's lightness of touch and makes scones that are just as delicious and buttery as her grandmother's. I use the same recipe, but still mine are more like rock cakes. However, I have managed to achieve one failsafe recipe, and it received the highest praise from a visiting preacher once, which is my claim to fame as far as baking goes.

On this particular occasion, the Harvest Thanksgiving

service was being held in the evening. We thought 8.30 p.m. was perfect timing, as we wouldn't have to rush to get there. We arrived at   8.28 p.m. and thought it was rather strange that everyone was inside already. We left the plates of sliced biscuit cake covered with cling film on the table in the outer room and went into the church. Every pew was full, so we took a seat upstairs. It was clearly not the beginning of the service – in fact, the clergyman announced the closing hymn! In our defence, apparently it was announced initially as 8.30 p.m. but then had changed to 7.30 p.m.

As I hadn't helped out in the decorating of the church bar a vase of arranged flowers and a basket of vegetables, nor had I made it to the service, I thought I'd better make myself useful and parked myself at the sink for the washing up. I was elbow deep in suds and mugs when someone came in to ask if they could wrap up my remaining biscuit cake to give to the guest preacher to bring home. I said yes of course, and didn't think anything more about it.

Everyone was called back into the church as the preacher wanted to say a few words and thank everyone for their hospitality. His next sentence made me want to sink through the floor as he waxed lyrical about his love for biscuit cake, how he hadn't tasted biscuit cake as nice for years and he was delighted to be bringing some home to his wife, as she loved it too.

Maybe I have underestimated my baking abilities after all! I guess another of my children's childhood memories will be of their mother making biscuit cake for every and any event.

17

PUSS IN BOOTS

Most farms tend to have feral cats and the numbers here vary from year to year. They earn their keep by killing vermin and are rewarded with as much milk as they want to drink and scraps of food. In the evenings, when they know the dogs are in bed, they come out of their hiding places among the straw bales and sneak across to the calf shed where they lap at creamy milk. Some cats are quite daring and if I leave a bucket of milk in the calf shed for a few minutes I'll return to see them drinking from it, doing their best not to fall in.

When I was a child, we had a tortoiseshell cat who was the matriarch for years. She was extremely elegant with mixed markings of black, red and gold. Others came and went; she always stayed. While other cats were too wild to let us near them, she used to wander into the milking parlour and calf sheds, and while she never stopped to be petted, she allowed me to run my hand along her back and the length of her tail before walking on with great poise. It was as if the milking parlour was her catwalk. Occasionally she had a litter of kittens, and there was huge excitement the year we found five of her kittens at the top of the straw bales. She didn't mind us playing with them and, indeed, seemed to see us as babysitters, as she would head off to do some hunting whenever we arrived. For many weeks, we climbed up the staggered bales to the row at the top, where we played with the kittens only feet from the roof.

More stray cats came and went. The occasional one stayed for life. We never encouraged them to come down around the house but one cat was persistent. She was fairly tame and we suspected she had been dumped out of a car. I was allergic to cats so she wasn't allowed into the house. One day, she disappeared out of the blue. The following weekend, I happened to mention that a cat with similar colouring arrived at the boarding school during the week. Then the penny dropped and we realised what had happened. The previous Sunday evening she must have hopped into the boot when I was packing up the car. When we arrived at the school, she jumped out and wasn't noticed. The following morning she made her presence known and had a huge fuss made of her by numerous schoolgirls. We didn't try to get her back, reckoning she'd have a better life where she could become a firm favourite with lots of boarding girls and staff and be well fed with titbits.

About ten years ago, a marmalade tomcat stayed for a couple of years. He left marmalade kittens in his wake and disappeared for about a year. When he returned, he was thin, battered and bruised, like he'd been in a few fights. He came down to the back door looking for food. There was a second tomcat on the farm by that point, a black and white one, and as soon as Mr Marmalade saw the other, he scarpered, clearly terrified. I used to stay standing over him while he ate, as if the other arrived, he bolted. Yet again, some marmalade and white kittens were born. He stayed with us for the rest of his life, eventually becoming thin and gaunt, and dying of old age.

We have one particular cat at the moment, who is an excellent mother and mouser. The only problem is that she seems to prefer her rats matured and it's not overly pleasant to walk into a shed and see a dead rat on the ground. She leaves it for about twenty-four hours before bringing it to her kittens.

It's interesting to watch the mother cats training their kittens. They bring them out to play and watch from a distance, allowing them independence but still being there to protect. They train them to run if a human or dog appears, ensuring they remain wary for life.

I deliberately don't make pets of them as I've learnt that tamer cats twist themselves around my wellies and it's not so convenient when I'm carrying a couple of full buckets of milk. They know where to find food and milk. They aren't pampered but have a good independent life in the barn.

18

CHRISTMASES PAST AND PRESENT

Christmas, a religious festival, also involved some rather pagan beliefs. It was believed that on Christmas night farm animals talked to each other in voices that humans could understand. However, it's bad luck to hear them and allegedly anyone who has visited a cowshed or stable to listen, and has heard them chatting about his/her demise, had died within the next week.

Christmas Day in the 1940s and 1950s was similar to a Sunday, but with even more food. The house would be decorated with holly and ivy just a couple of days previously. My grandmother Lily would rear a number of turkeys so that they had their own home-reared bird and the usual visitors to help eat it all. She used to send a turkey in the post to her sister; I remember hearing about people posting fried eggs between sheets of newspaper during the war. At a time when food was rationed and scarce, farmers had a bountiful Christmas. They produced their own bird, vegetables and potatoes. Even though Lily made a huge Christmas cake,

Charlie always brought her up a shop-bought one too, perfectly iced. While the beauty of the icing was always admired, the highest praise always went to the homebaked one. A huge round plum pudding was served with custard after dinner. Christmas gifts were limited but the children got dinky toys and balloons in their stockings, usually broken or burst by dinner time.

On St Stephen's Day – Boxing Day – the wren boys came out in force. Young men, and occasionally women, dressed up in old clothes, painted their faces and sometimes wore straw hats. They went from house to house playing music, dancing and accepting money while also chanting:

'The wren, the wren, the king of all birds
On St Stephen's Day it was caught in the furze
Up with the kettle and down with the pan
Given me a penny to bury the wren.'

The less savoury aspect of their activities was the killing of a wren and displaying it. Why a wren? It is alleged that it is a treacherous bird, and it betrayed St Stephen, the first Christian martyr, by flapping its wings and alerting his pursuers. A wren was also alleged to have alerted Cromwell's troops to the presence of Irish forces about to attack. The practice continues in some parts of the country still, but now they use a fake bird, or usually just a small sod of turf on the end of a stick to denote the dead wren.

When Dad was young, just like on a Sunday, only the bare minimum of work was done. Two or three cows was all that needed to be milked as the rest were dry. Animals were fed and bedded before everyone went to church and they took life easy for the afternoon. When I was a child, Christmas week always seemed relaxed. Most visiting to and by relations had been completed in the run up to Christmas, the food and decorating preparations were finished and, as a child, my favourite activity was lying on the rug in front of the fire reading all the books I'd received. We would ice the cake a few days before Christmas. One year, the phone rang when we were in the middle of doing it, so my sister Daphne and I continued icing while Mum chatted in the hall. We were dipping the flat knife in boiling water to smooth the icing but to such an extent the icing kept sliding off the cake onto the table. We kept scooping it back up. Needless to say, the cake didn't have a smooth finish that year.

Christmas Eve is often the day that farmers go shopping. Sometimes Dad went to the jewellery shop after going to the mart earlier in the month. There was one salesperson who was able to advise husbands exactly what they had bought their wives on previous occasions and which bracelet or earrings was perfect to finish the set. Of course, I'd imagine the wives had also called in some weeks previously to choose what they wanted, just in case their husbands did go shopping.

Farm salesmen called up on Christmas Eve or a few days previously, perhaps hoping for another order before the festive period but also to say thank you for the purchases during the year. As my parents were teetotallers, they didn't receive bottles of whisky, but I do remember boxes of liqueur chocolates. The salesmen always gave a calendar too, so the kitchen walls were adorned with all sorts of calendars with pictures of cows, horses, machinery and local scenes. The bottles of whisky from salesmen have started making a reappearance again recently; we received three last

Christmas. The postman always got a Christmas box and as the drink-driving laws were more relaxed then, he got a drink in many houses along his round.

When Dad came in on Christmas Eve night, he was besieged with questions about how much hay he had left on the roof for the reindeer and we poured Father Christmas a glass of Lucozade and cut him the first slice from the Christmas cake before going to bed.

We were allowed to open our gifts from Father Christmas in the morning. We crept down to get our presents from under the tree and, if up very early, often returned to bed with our books to read for an hour before getting up for breakfast. One year I got a portable typewriter and lots of Hardy Boys books; I was in heaven. We went to church for 11 a.m. and our visitors arrived in time for lunch at 1 p.m. Farming neighbours, John and Kate O'Neill, who always found Christmas a lonely day, came up to us for over thirty years. My sister's godparents came up as well. All other gifts were opened around 3 p.m. when we were all seated in the sitting room after dinner. The 'good room' was used for occasions such as Christmas Day and as it didn't have a television, the focus was on conversation, jokes and board games. The only change from when Dad was a child was that they always listened to the King's Speech. The dinner had to be eaten and cleared away so everyone could cluster around the radio to listen at 3 p.m. I wasn't even aware of the Queen's Speech, as we never listened to it. Our visitors wouldn't have been interested, so it wouldn't have been appropriate to switch on the radio.

Christmas hasn't changed much over the years, despite the increase in hype about it. Perhaps because of the hype that goes on for months, we try to do the opposite and have a quiet time. If anything, I'm much more relaxed than my mum was, or I should say I don't make as much effort. The decorations go up around the 15th of December. Any earlier and I'd be so tired of looking at them that I'd be itching to take them down by St Stephen's Day. We each open one present on Christmas Eve and sometimes we go to church at midnight. On Christmas morning, the children wake around 6 a.m. and gifts from Father Christmas are opened and played with. The fire is lit and we have mugs of tea and chocolates from one of the many tins of sweets. The turkey is put in the oven and then ignored for a few hours. Brian goes to check on the livestock and push in some silage and then it's off to church. Sometimes we have family here, sometimes we spend the day alone just the four of us, playing board games, building Lego and bringing the dogs for a walk. The livestock get another check before teatime, but Brian likes to get outdoors for a while in any case.

I think farmers are secretly glad to get out to the cool air and the peace and quiet of the sheds for a little while, to escape from the heat of the 'good rooms' and the incessant noise of new games and excited children. One would be forgiven for thinking the animals are in a peaceful and contemplative mood too, as they seem to quietly respect the birth of Christ in their own way. As the yard is quiet – no callers, no loader beeping as it reverses, no tractor noises, no drone from the milking parlour – their thoughts aren't interrupted by the sound of day-to-day farm life. The animals were double foddered on Christmas Eve so they are also sleepy, like the humans, after lots of food. Most are lying down and the occasional one lifts a head to stare at the farmer while chewing its cud and another one strolls slowly to the water trough. They will be back to normal on St Stephen's Day, but on our farm, where we don't milk from around 20 December to 1 February, Christmas Day is a day of quiet reflection and rest for man, woman and beast.

19

THAT'S A LOAD OF BULL

The success of any dairy or beef farm lies in the calves. Without calves, no milk would be produced, nor would there be any young cows to add to the herd. Getting cows in calf isn't necessarily that straightforward. Bulls can be temporarily infertile, for example. In the mid-twentieth century, not every farm had a bull and artificial insemination was only starting to become popular. Even with the increased use of A.I. now, a bull is kept on most dairy or beef farms. Most farms these days use A.I. for the first six weeks of the breeding season and a pedigree stock bull to 'clean up'. The bull is either let out into the field with the cows or any cow showing signs of ovulating spends time with the bull in his 'boudoir'. Cows ovulate every three weeks but will show signs of 'coming on heat' the day before.

Bulls can be very dangerous animals. Some breeds tend to be quieter than others, but they are all capable of killing a person. Some of our bulls have been quite fractious. There is an echo in our yard, so when a bull bellows and hears his own echo, he thinks there is another bull nearby ready to take him on and threaten his ownership of the harem.

Bulls can kill with a toss of the head and years ago their horns made them even more dangerous. Nowadays, unless a specialist breed, they are dehorned soon after birth. In 1901, a man was severely gored by a bull on this farm, and he later died of his injuries. John Scully worked as a coachman and groom for Hubert Warren and one day he went to assist Brown, the herdsman, who was taking the bull out of his stall. The bull attacked both of them. Brown was thrown behind the gate, but Scully bore the brunt of his horns. He suffered a large gaping wound in his abdomen and, although a doctor attended, he died from his wounds the same day.[7]

WHAT'S IN A NAME?

Bulls have a significant presence on the farm. They are treated with respect and some affection because of their size, their importance to the future of the herd and their personality traits. They are usually housed on their own in a shed or a paddock with good, strong fencing. As bovines are herd animals, they are quite sociable and need the company of others, so should be able to see and smell other bovines. They need their daily chat with others. I find it's normal to have a chat with a bull as I pass by, even if it is just a cheery hello or a grunt. You might be looked at askance if seen talking to yourself, but you can get away with chatting to livestock. Hence, it's not uncommon for breeding bulls to be called a pet name, sometimes a shortened version of their pedigree name.

The length of time a bull is kept on a farm depends on a number of factors. Is he quiet or ferocious? Is his fertility good? Is he throwing good-quality offspring and are they easy calving? If the bulls are being kept for more than a year, we always give them names. The name usually reflects their colouring, size or personality.

We bought two Rotbundt bulls when we took over the farm in 2003. Good for beef and milk, these are a broad muscular animal with dark red and creamy white colouring. The first was called R.B. He was quiet but firm. As long as we weren't going to fool around in his presence – as if we would – he tolerated us. He reminded me of a mature and slightly disapproving teacher, as he certainly gave the impression he was going to frown upon any silly or immature behaviour. He demanded respect and he wasn't going to be ordered around. Like many animals, he liked company and routine. He had a chat with the cows when he saw them coming in to be milked. Once they'd gone out to the field, he wasn't happy if we forgot to open the gate to let him saunter from his pen – called the bull's house – to the cubicles to get water. He developed a knack of using his tongue to pull the latch back on another gate, so it had to be tied to prevent him going walkabout.

Buster, the younger Rotbundt, was a lighter bull. With more spring in his step, he seemed livelier and cheekier. But he became much more wicked as time went on, so wasn't with us for as long. They both gave us wonderful daughters and we still have a couple in the milking herd. We remember them both with affection.

Other bulls have had human names. A few of our bulls were genotyped by A.I. companies and didn't make their grade, but we kept them as our stock bulls for a single season. Sometimes a calf just looks like a Barry or a Fred and keeps the name as he moves into adulthood. In 2010, one of our bull calves was purchased by an A.I. company. We didn't realise we could have named him and discovered they had given him the charming name of Lucifer. This wasn't exactly what we had in mind for the cute white and black calf heading off into potential stardom. I felt a name signifying the evil of Satan wasn't going to bode well for his temperament.

A.I. companies accepted two more bulls over the next couple of years. As my first books touched on the subjects of love and marriage, and hoping lots of romance was in the air for these young bulls, we called the second one Matchmaker and the third one Bachelor.

This year, two breeding bulls and a vasectomised bull – known as a 'teaser' – had been used for one season and were being fattened in the calving shed, which has a big sliding door to one side. It's an old shed and it can be hard to get the door to slide back and fasten properly when the straw and dung build up. I was indoors when I got a phone call from Brian during milking to say the bulls were out. It was dark and I hadn't a clue where I was going to find them. Would they have headed towards the road? Would they have gone up the yard and be on the way to the fields? Were the gates closed on the fields?

Luckily, they hadn't gone far. One was still in the shed looking out the door as if to say, 'I'd prefer to stay in here if it's all the same to you.' One was in the empty calf shed next door and another had wandered up the yard. Grabbing pitchforks to be on the safe side, it was easy enough to get them back in. The door was then secured with wire as well as rope. We called the bull that was up the yard Houdini.

Houdini lived up to his name. One morning, I walked past their pen first thing and did a double take as there were only two bulls there. Houdini was missing – escaped. I looked around: no sign of any breakouts, although there was a lot of straw strewn around the feeding passage. More importantly, there was no sign of a bull at large. I checked the cow house opposite and found him fastened in there temporarily. Brian had found him in the feeding passage at 6 a.m. He had tossed a couple of straw bales around and was lying on a comfy bed. We couldn't work out how he got out. I tested each of the rungs in the feeding barrier to see if any had come loose and been his escape route. All seemed secure. Perhaps he had jumped the feeding barrier, but it's very high so that seemed unlikely. We put him back with the others and decided to close all the yard gates every night and when we were away during the day so he wouldn't get far even if he did escape again.

And guess what? He did. Again, I got a phone call from Brian to say Houdini was out and sauntering around the yard. I armed myself with a pitchfork – not that I expected to have to use it, but I prefer to be armed in case I need it to deflect a large head coming towards me. This time, it was easy to work out what he'd done. The far side of the sliding door had been pushed out and hadn't slipped back into place. Once we got him back in, more security measures were applied to that side of the door and he didn't escape again.

We now have a beef breed bull, a Hereford. They are mostly dark red in colour with a white head and some white markings. Our newly purchased bull had a white stripe on one side so we named him Flash. Unfortunately, he was a bit of a flash in the pan and didn't cut a dash with the cows at all. First of all, his ardour seemed low – non-existent really. We were accustomed to Friesian bulls who would mount anything that stood still. Even though we allowed him to acclimatise to his surroundings for a few days and let only a single cow in with him in his boudoir, he seemed intimidated by the black and white cows. When we peeked in, the cow was staring at us as if to say, 'What am I supposed to do to attract this handsome chap?' while Flash stood beside her, totally oblivious to her charms.

Two days later, a red and white cow was on heat and her colour, being similar to his, seemed to make him more comfortable and he realised what he was supposed to be doing. However, three weeks later, some cows started coming on heat again; this was a surprise as we were convinced they would be in calf. Their tag numbers corresponded to those who had been with Flash. He had been fertility tested, but after speaking to the seller, we got him tested again. The first test was fine but the second test showed he was temporarily infertile.

The seller replaced him with another bull. This one's pedigree name is Indestructible, which made us more hopeful. His semen was tested twice and all was positive. A shortened name like Indie seemed too soft for this fifteen-month-old bull who would grow to an impressively big stature. I wanted to call him Sebastian, but Brian kept forgetting this name so now he's simply called Red. He's friendly and placid, and as long as he has silage in front of him he's a happy boy. He doesn't overexert himself but gets the job done. He's very relaxed, like an old man who enjoys having a cigar and brandy in front of the fire instead of doing any work.

We also have Tweedledum and Tweedledee. As you can

probably guess by their names, these were the runts of the year rather than being two fine things. They are twins, both small, and were the last-born calves of their year. They both succumbed to cryptosporidium and needed a lot of nursing for their first couple of months. They were housed separately to the other calves, as they were so much smaller. They had each other for company and were content. We left them entire – meaning that we didn't castrate them – to give them a bit more potential for growing and building muscle, but there was no possibility of them being fattened by sixteen months, which is the age our other bulls go for beef.

We decided to vasectomise them. They'd have a lively and fun summer and they'd be earning their keep. As 'teasers' they went out into the field with the breeding heifers once the first three weeks of A.I. was over and their job was to bring our attention to any heifers on heat. The bulls wear a 'chin ball', which means we can spot any cows on heat by the streaks of vivid pink paint on their backs. We did consider keeping them to use for a second year but Tweedledum has been starting to act too possessively near his harem, standing up to me for a few seconds too long, so they'll be off to the factory once they are ready.

Bulls are sometimes renamed to something like 'you evil sod' if kept too long. These two were never dehorned, as they were so poorly that we didn't want to put them through it. There was some superstition at play here too, that if we dehorned them, they'd be bound to die the next week. So now we refer to them, aptly, as the 'horny lads'.

We find that with all the talk of cows being on heat, bulls not working at all or working well, and semen test results, farm children get a very pragmatic view of bovine conception.

THE ILLEGAL BULL

In the 1950s, all bulls had to be licensed. A countrywide effort was underway to improve the quality of the livestock. Farmers received a subsidy if their licensed bull was available to service other farmers' cows. Isaac Langrell, a farmer two miles away, had a licensed Shorthorn bull. He charged fifteen shillings for the bull's services to get a cow in calf.

The cow had to be brought to his farm, but it wasn't as straightforward as it sounds. First of all, the timing had to be right. The cow had to be observed to be on heat. Some cows present very obvious signs: they tend to be flighty, move around a lot and will try to mount any other cow that stands for them. Nowadays, once she has been noticed, it's just a case of letting her into the bull's quarters, but in the 1950s at Garrendenny the cow had to be walked the two miles to Langrell's farm.

She was escorted across a large field to reach the road, down a narrow country lane and then along the main road. A normally docile cow could be extremely temperamental when on heat. With hormones coursing through her veins, knowing she was on the way to meet her Romeo, a matronly old dear was capable of acting like a skittish young one. She would detour around the field, jump around the bundages (bunches of briars in the middle of the field), the clumps of rushes and the dykes within that large field. On reaching the farm, she was introduced to the bull and, if all went well, she became pregnant.

Dad bought their first bull in the early 1960s. An acquaintance, Herbert Fennell, had bred a number of Friesian bulls but something had been missed on the paperwork and one bull wasn't licensed. When it came to the time for him to be sold, Herbert had to choose between selling him as an unlicensed bull and keeping it quiet or fattening him for the factory. Dad paid £72 for this fine specimen, which was a very keen price due to his 'illegal status'.

Once the breeding season was over, the bull was put into a shed at the rear of the yard and the workman was warned that his presence had to be kept a secret. If anyone enquired if we had a bull, he had to deny it at all costs.

One day, Herbert was passing the gate and decided to call up and see how his bull was doing. Dad was away but on meeting the workman he enquired about the bull and was surprised to hear the bull didn't exist.

'But I sold Joe a bull,' he said.

'There ain't no bull here,' the workman insisted.

Eventually, Herbert convinced him that he was the previous owner of the unlicensed bull and understood the need for secrecy, and he got to see his bull.

NEVER THE TWAIN SHALL MEET

Bulls can be kept together if they are already accustomed to each other. They usually decide their own pecking order. One asserts his authority and is the boss. Problems can arise if they both want to be top dog, as they will fight until one capitulates. We keep the breeding bulls apart, partly for ease of managing them and partly to prevent any potential fighting and risk of injury.

Occasionally, bulls kept separately manage to get to each other. Last year, one of the breeding bulls got the door of the bull's house open and decided to go for an evening stroll with his current sweetheart. Our breeding heifers were in a field at the top of the yard with Tweedledum, the young vasectomised bull. Although he wasn't going to get any of them pregnant, he has all the testosterone and temper of an entire bull. He was small, only two-thirds the size of the other one. Hearing the other bull's bellow, he marched down the field, full of confidence and ready to protect his right to his harem. It reminded me of that popular image of a cat looking into a mirror and seeing a lion. Tweedledum obviously thought he was capable of beating the other bull to a pulp, watched by adoring female fans.

Fences and gates would normally be secure enough to keep them separate but, as we had been doing some building work, there was only a temporary electric fence in place. It wasn't going to be strong enough to keep them apart if they decided to have a spat. Just in time, Kate and I got the cow to turn around to send her back to the yard and the bigger bull was happy to follow his beloved.

When I was about eight years old, two bulls, 'the Auld Lad' and 'the Boss', got into a situation that could have killed them both. At three and five years of age, they were fully mature and viewed each other as arch enemies from their sheds at either end of the yard. They could hear each other bellow but couldn't see each other. Similar in height, the older was heavier but the younger was fitter. The Boss, the younger bull, was on the way back to his house after being in the cattle crush for a tuberculosis test when the Auld Lad managed to knock down the gate of his shed. He charged across the yard. He pushed against the Boss, who pushed back. A mammoth black head against a colossal black and white head, they tussled as men shouted and grabbed pitchforks. Focused on each other, they were oblivious to the humans.

The heavier bull, the Auld Lad, was pushing the Boss back further and further. Behind him was a five-bar gate but behind that was the dungsted. The slurry and dung was about five feet deep at that point. The Boss was pushed against the old gate. His weight made it fall back, the thick skin on top of the slurry cracked and a huge brown splash went up into the air. Pushing him into the slurry wasn't enough. The Auld Lad wasn't going to just stand there and lord it as king of the castle from the height of the yard. He jumped in with a roar, nearly landing on top of the other bull.

As they fought, they moved further out into the dungsted, where it was even deeper. Was this going to be a similar end to the legendary fight between the Brown Bull of Cooley and the white bull belonging to Queen Medb's husband Aillil? In that story, the white bull was killed and parts of him were thrown to the four corners of Ireland. Would one kill the other? Would they both drown in the slurry? Would they see sense and move towards the shallow end and get out?

Ladders and gates were put on top of the slurry from the other side, men climbed on and shouted at the bulls, but they weren't paying any attention. They were focused on trying to kill. At one point, they were in the deepest part and all we could see of them were their noses as they sank again and again. Every now and then, one got a huge surge of energy and he'd emerge with a roar, his skin covered with brown slime as he tried to submerge the other one. Then both would flounder again.

All we could do was leave them struggling and fighting and go to the outfarm to finish the tuberculosis test on the cattle there. The gate was left open and we hoped that they would make their way to it and get out.

They fought for hours and eventually both bulls made their way to the gateway. The Auld Lad climbed out first and stood there, shaking, hungry, tired and filthy. He didn't put up any protest when he was urged into his shed. The Boss followed within fifteen minutes and got the same treatment. Separate houses, fastened in with strong gates, fresh silage, some ration for energy, fresh water and rest.

NEVER TRUST A BULL

When I was a child, we kept our Friesian bulls for a few seasons. Friesians are often viewed as the most unpredictable of the bull breeds and Mum was always worried a bull would get out of his shed. Even though they looked docile, I knew from a very early age that meeting a bull in the yard might not end well. I grew up with the 'never trust a bull' mantra and gave them a very wide berth.

When I was about ten years old, we borrowed a bull from a neighbour for part of the breeding season. Rather than letting a cow on heat in to the bull as we do now, he was let out with the cows. As he was a bit temperamental, I wasn't allowed to go for the cows on my own. On this particular day, work had run late and it was decided Tommy and I would bring the cows in while Dad got the milking parlour ready. The cows were in Lynup's Hill, a nearby field with a particularly steep hill up to a quarry on the top. Tommy, with his long strides and probably keen to finish work and get home, went on ahead. He had reached the top of the hill when I was only about halfway up.

As sometimes happened, some cows, instead of strolling along, decided it was good fun to canter and buck. A white cow appeared over the brow of the hill with the bull in quick pursuit. She kicked up her heels and ran down about thirty feet until she was level with me. The bull came along to the other side of her. Both stopped and looked at me, his ring quivering in his nose. I couldn't move. They seemed fascinated by me and both stood there, staring, heads and tails high in the air. They even seemed mildly amused to be teasing or tormenting me; I wasn't sure which.

After what was seconds but felt like minutes, I found my legs and my voice. 'Tommyyy,' I squeaked as I started running up the hill. The cow decided she'd had enough and took off to join her comrades. The bull thought she was more interesting to follow than I was. Standing in the middle of the field without sticks was probably a tad silly but as we walked back down, me behind Tommy, the bull was standing his ground and staring at us. Tommy lifted a clod of earth and threw it at him, which persuaded the bull to move off.

I was told afterwards by a neighbour that a bull standing and staring didn't mean he was going to attack. The warning signs are pawing the ground, snorting and lowering his head as if to charge. I wasn't convinced or reassured. It struck me that it would have taken him only seconds to lower his head and then run at me. I wasn't sorry when he was returned to his owner.

I was reminded of this incident when our daughter stood up to a bull. She was eleven years old and was helping Brian to move the breeding heifers and Barry, the bull, from one field to another. Brian went to gather up the cattle with Sam, our dog, while Kate was 'stopping a gap' to ensure they went towards the gateway. She had a stick as a precaution but Brian wasn't concerned. Barry was only sixteen months and up to now had been very quiet.

As soon as Barry saw Kate, he took exception to her. He didn't remember her from when she fed him milk as a young calf. He was about eight feet away from her, shaking his head, roaring and frothing at the mouth. Brian, being some distance away, tried to get Sam to intervene, but he didn't understand and Brian didn't want to risk sending Barry closer to Kate so he stopped trying. Brian was calling to her to hold her ground but to slowly move closer to the electric fence – still about twenty feet away – so she could dive in under it. She didn't hear him and was waving her stick with defiance and determination, telling Barry to move along. Just as Brian got there, Barry capitulated and moved off with his heifers. On asking Kate why she hadn't moved closer to the wire, she replied, 'He didn't seem to want to move off but I wasn't going to let him win.'

Maybe I should have been chanting the 'never trust a bull' mantra more often. I know I can be stubborn, hot-headed and determined, but at least I know when it's sensible to give in. While I admired Kate's steadfastness and determination, I got a shock when I heard what she had done. Sometimes you have to know when to let others – people or animals – win a battle, knowing you will win the war in the long run.

The problem is that when you have fed a tiny bull calf by bottle, and given it a name, you always have a soft spot for it. It can be too easy to believe that it likes you too, that it remembers you being so kind to it, and that it would never hurt you. But even though he may not mean to cause injury – he may just be curious or playful, – a bull can still injure with just a toss of the head.

We had three Friesian bulls housed together while being fattened. They seemed docile enough. I rubbed their heads at

221

the feeding barrier, I chatted to them while giving them ration and silage. The black bull was the boss, yet at times the other two turned on him. It may have been tomfoolery and it may have been half-serious fighting, but within seconds one day the other two had the black bull down on his back with his legs up in the air scrabbling to find ground. If they can do that to one of their own kind, they could really decimate a person in seconds. Yes, I did double-check the strength of the feeding barrier that's been there for years and was dividing me from them. 'Never trust a bull' is a good lesson to remember.

20

NOT ONLY CATS
HAVE NINE LIVES

I think all people do stupid things without realising it at one time or another. Sometimes they will weigh up the risks and reckon it is perfectly safe but something goes wrong. Sometimes people use up every one of their nine lives during the course of their long lifetime and get away with it. Unfortunately, though, it still happens that farming accidents result in loss of life, and farming is now one of the most dangerous occupations. It's not just working farmers who are losing lives; often it is young children or retired farmers. No one seems to know how to prevent all these accidents, although various ideas have been voiced.

Dad definitely took risks in the past, probably like so many other farmers out there, believing he was invincible and would get away with it. One day in the late 1960s Dad and Tommy had sown some beech trees, but they had also cut down and chopped up some old trees that were in danger of falling in the next storm. Dad had driven the Massey Ferguson 135 and trailer off the track to get nearer to the pile of sawn logs. They filled the trailer but as he had gone down the hill too far, the tractor couldn't get back up along the rough ground to the track. It was too steep with too many hollows and stumps of trees blocking the way. It was getting close to milking time and patience was probably in short supply. The only way out was down the extremely steep slope. He decided he'd jump off the tractor if it started to slide down the hill; he had no wish to be on something that felt like a rollercoaster ride gone wrong. As the tractor started along the downward slope, he steered the tractor towards a small section of level ground, but the tractor wheels started to slide. He jumped off, knocking the tractor out of gear as he went. Luckily, the trailer wheel hit a stump and that stopped the tractor in its tracks. Dad got back up and managed to drive down the rest of the steep hill to safety. Bonkers, yes.

One year, he was spreading dung in the Big Field on the outfarm. He had already transported the dung over with a tipping trailer, and it was piled in a huge heap in the adjoining field. The Zetor tractor was pulling the dung spreader and he was using the Massey Ferguson to load the spreader with dung. He was working away happily on his own until the battery went down on the Zetor and it stopped working.

He knew he could get it started if the Zetor got a push but how was he to do that on his own? He couldn't push it with the Massey Ferguson and yet be in the Zetor to drive it too. He could have walked to a neighbour's farm and asked him to come and sit on the Zetor for a minute, but that would have taken time and he can be impatient. He left the Zetor in gear so it would start when pushed. He got on the Massey Ferguson and drove it forward so it pushed the dung spreader and the other tractor. As the Zetor started spluttering into life, he stopped the Massey Ferguson and jumped off, running as fast as he could to the Zetor, which was making its way slowly down the field. As he neared it, the Zetor gave a puff of smoke and accelerated. He grabbed the handle of the sliding door (it had been left open) and jumped up on the steps just in time. A second later and he would have been left looking after a driverless tractor heading down the field towards the ditch.

Quite rightly, regulations regarding the roadworthiness of vehicles have tightened considerably. Tractors require good lighting and trailers or other implements need to have working lights too. While cattle used to be walked along the road to fairs, to the mart and to our outfarm, or transported in small trailers, they are now always taken in cattle trailers or lorries. Regulations weren't always so strict. In the 1970s, Dad used to bring cows and calves to the mart on the same day, using one tractor and two trailers.

Did he go twice?

No. This was multi-tasking at its finest.

First of all the small cattle trailer was hitched to the Zetor tractor and four cows were loaded into it – four was its maximum capacity. The pig trailer, which was low but high enough to take calves, was hitched to the back of the cattle trailer, and loaded with calves. It was secured to the other trailer with a pin and tied with baler twine for good measure. Off he went with two trailers, one behind the other.

When he arrived at the mart, it was just a case of unloading the calves, unhitching that trailer and pushing it out of the way before unloading the cows. The trailers never unhitched from each other and it was viewed as being an efficient use of time and facilities. I don't think anyone would risk it now!

I was about seven or eight when I had my first trailer mishap. I was travelling the two miles to the outfarm with Tommy and as he was driving the Massey Ferguson, which had neither a passenger seat nor space to stand, I opted to sit on the trailer. Tommy told me to make sure I stayed in the middle, not to go near the edge, and I was sitting there contented, watching the world go by, almost feeling like I was watching it in reverse and enjoying the gentle rumble of the motion of the trailer.

As the tractor started the descent down the narrow road at Killeen, the pace picked up. The rumbles intensified to a number of jolts, and I found out I had a coccyx as it bounced off the hard wood of the trailer. I scrambled to my knees when the trailer grated to a stop and saw Tommy driving on, leaving me behind in the middle of the road. Would the trailer stay still now or would it take off down the steep hill towards the bridge and over the wall to the river? I shouted his name and whether he heard me, sensed something was wrong or just looked around to check on me, he turned his head, and I realised the expression 'his eyes nearly fell out of their sockets' was accurate. He did a double take before hitting the brakes and reversing back to me. Never one to be dramatic, though, he told me I was perfectly safe, searched around for the missing pin and found it, got a large stone and managed to lift the drawbar of the trailer onto it, then hitched up again. Needless to say, the rest of my journey was completed on the tractor.

We used to love getting rides in John O'Neill's transport box during haymaking time. One summer it was decided that we would go for a picnic, up the hills to Rossmore, and travel there in the transport box. John's sister Kate, Mum, we three children and our cousin Jonathan sat on the straw bale in the transport box as the tractor trundled up the road. We could have gone in the car, of course, but it was the transport that made the day so memorable. The straw scratched our legs, the transport box bobbed up and down, we enjoyed travelling with our backs to our destination and seeing a different view. Having had the picnic, we were excited to find pieces of coal around the mouth to a coalpit and insisted on throwing some into the transport box to bring home. We picked frockins (wild blueberries) but once we tasted them, our enthusiasm for picking waned. Would children be permitted to travel in a transport box nowadays? No.

A few years ago, a fox got into our outdoor slurry tank somehow. Now, the tank has a shed over it, but back then it had a high fence all around it. The tank was eight feet deep and it had about four feet of slurry in it, topped with a dry crust. The fox was light enough to be able to run on top of the crust. He wasn't able to find his way out. We put down a long board and hoped he'd make his way back to it but that didn't work. We weren't going to risk our own lives by getting into the tank. We wouldn't have wanted to see him shot but, in any case, we don't have a gun so couldn't put him out of his misery. We didn't want to see him starve to death. We rang the ISPCA to ask their advice and they said they'd call out the following day. As it happened, it was Will's birthday and we'd planned to go to the zoo, so we didn't get to see how they managed it, but we came home to see a few pallets near the slurry tank and the fox was nowhere to be seen. It's always best to get in the experts, I guess.

Cows are wonderfully gentle creatures but their size

means that they are potential killers, even if they don't mean to be. One morning, Brian was bringing in the cows from the Letterbox field. They were walking up along a steep fenced track to the milking parlour. Some had already reached the yard and Brian was strolling behind the last cows. Suddenly he became aware of a commotion – the cows at the front were turning around and racing back down. This panicked the cows behind, who then also turned around. All he could do was jump over the wire to the field beside and get out of the way as they all galloped back down the hill.

Luckily, some of the cows broke through a stretch of wire to their left and filed into that field. The dogs didn't know what to think. Sam slunk off home, either giving up on it all or thinking he was in trouble. Lou looked at Brian, waiting to hear what she should do. He let them all calm down before rounding them up again. It might have been something as simple as a cat going across the path of the front cows, but the danger was that if Brian hadn't got out of the way so quickly, some of the cows, with nowhere else to go, would have trampled him.

21

DAD'S LITTLE HELPER

When I think back over my childhood in terms of farming, it is Dad who features in most of my memories. Even though I wasn't the kind of kid who lived for farming – I lived for books, to be honest – I spent a lot of time with him, because he was a farmer. He was always at home; all I had to do was go out on the farm to find him.

It's more difficult now for busy farmers to do the childcare. Machinery is bigger and more dangerous. There aren't as many jobs where children can just tag along and help out. On Saturday afternoons, when Dad was continually walking to and from the hayshed to the little cow houses with small square bales of straw, I trailed after him. Sheds and bales are much larger now and the lifting work is done by large machinery. It's against Irish law for children under seven to ride on a tractor, even with a seat belt, which many feel is throwing out the baby with the bathwater, as they argue the safest place is often on the tractor. I certainly wouldn't recommend that you have small children with you when unrolling a large bale of straw in a shed full of cattle either.

Whenever Mum announced she had to go to town, there was always an immediate clamour of, 'Dad, what are you and Tommy doing today?' It was bad enough having to go to town for essential purchases like shoes and clothes, but I hated having to go grocery shopping or to the bank, which meant trailing after Mum on the high street, where she seemed to know everyone and stopped continuously for conversations. My children tell me I seem to know everyone too, and as I'd say I have at most one conversation per town visit, perhaps my memories are deceiving me. But if there was anything the men were doing where we could tag along, we much preferred that.

We had two tractors. The Massey Ferguson was a disaster as far as children was concerned, as it didn't have a passenger seat, the mudguards were much too narrow to sit on, and there was very little floor space to stand. The Zetor was great: there was a passenger seat and two wide interior mudguards as seats. More often than not then, we spent the afternoon on the Zetor tractor spreading fertiliser or dung or slurry. I remember them as nice lazy afternoons, but I'm sure we said 'I'm bored' on a few occasions too. I used to stand on the drawbar behind the tractor sometimes when Dad was pulling the large roller behind the Ferguson. Apart from it being madness from a safety perspective, it must have been really monotonous. I would go herding with Dad from when I was a toddler, as apparently it was a way to distract me from scratching the rash on my arms and legs. It was a two-mile drive over to the outfarm and then a walk around the fields, counting and checking the cattle. Not that I did that much walking – I used to run in front of Dad and put my arms up to be carried. One of my earliest memories is of my dad stopping to chat to an old man who was pushing his old black bike laden with bags of groceries. I was slightly scared of him, as he was dressed totally in black, but remember that he tried to allay my fears by giving me ten pence to buy a bar of chocolate.

When I was young, accompanying either Dad or Tommy on the Saturday morning trip to the creamery with the milk tank was considered a nice excursion on a sunny day. There was always a queue when we got there. Thinking back, it was so time-consuming compared to the ten minutes it takes for the milk collector to take the milk now, but it meant that farmers could have a daily chat with neighbours. There was no need to feel any guilt about socialising either, as it was part of the working day; they just had to wait their turn. If the queue was long, we were sent up to the local shop to get a few sweets. I presume we were getting impatient and tetchy and it was a way to distract us.

If we were in bed when Dad got in from work, he had the job of telling us bedtime stories. My sister and I used to fight over whose bed he should sit on, so he usually kneeled on the floor between the two beds. I loved hearing stories of things he got up to when he was young. One of my favourites was when he offered his younger cousin a spin on his BSA 150 motorbike. They set off down the avenue and as Frances got off the bike to open the gates at the road my father sped off. She had to walk back up the hill to the castle; I'm sure she was absolutely fuming but she got her revenge. She cut lots of nettles and thistles and remade his bed for him. That night as he climbed under the covers he was nicely stung, and had to remake his bed with fresh sheets as the thorns were embedded in the fabric.

Going to the mart or factory was a treat too. My parents weren't the type to give us days off school too easily, but I remember once having to go to the dentist for a filling. Mum dropped me off and afterwards I walked up to the mart to meet Dad. I was perfectly happy watching calves being bought and sold, rounding off our morning's work with tea and a bun in the mart café.

Dad was a keen cyclist, just for fun, although he sometimes went on twenty-mile sponsored rides when racing bikes became popular. The five of us often went for a cycle on Sunday afternoons. The photographs are amusing when you compare us to what cyclists wear nowadays. My dad wore farming clothes all week, but he dressed up on a Sunday and therefore went cycling in good trousers and a sports jacket – reminding me those old photographs of men wearing suits at the beach. One of the best things about having a farmer for a dad was that he was always around. Farmers can get bad press for working long hours, and Dad certainly did that, but he was always either in the milking parlour, a field or the yard. It was a case of going for a walk and I'd soon find him. It's not always easy or sensible to let children wander off in search of their dad, of course.

We've always impressed on the children that we have to know where they are. Much depends on how far the house is from the farm. Our back garden backs onto the yard; it's only separated by a narrow band of deciduous trees, a fence and a garden gate. The proximity means it is easy for Brian to pop in, or for the children to go out with him for a run on the tractor or to bring in the cows. It also carries risks, in case they take a notion to go up to the farmyard – although we keep the gate closed, an adventurous child could climb the fence. Thank goodness they have always recognised that they must either get our permission or go with us.

One of Will's regular jobs in the springtime was giving ration to the calves. He used to fill his buckets in the meal house and saunter to the three calf sheds to pour the ration into the troughs or buckets there. The timing for this job usually coincided with Brian being close to finishing milking the cows. On so many occasions, as Brian collected his phone from the pump room after milking and was checking messages, in a world of his own, Will would sneak up and yell a loud 'Boo!' The higher Brian jumped, the louder Will's laugh. We'd hear him still laughing away in the calf shed five minutes later. One day, Brian decided to get his own back. It was dusky and when Will was busy in one calf shed, Brian sneaked into the meal shed and hid behind the sliding door. Only his wellies were visible from the yard. Will never noticed and as he walked in and Brian shouted 'Boo!', there was a loud shriek of terror. Brian had got his revenge. The two of them still play tricks like that on each other. They have a matching dimple in their right cheek and a very similar dry sense of humour.

There's no doubt that farming presents challenges for family life. It involves long hours, it can carry risks and it is often a tough, isolating lifestyle. However, farming also provides so many ways to spend time as a family. Indeed, farming families possibly spend more time together than others, as long as they are all out working together of course.

22

BEING NEIGHBOURLY

Farmers depended on their neighbours considerably in the past, there's no doubt about it. Farms were smaller, but farming was more labour intensive. Physical strength was needed in multiples of men (and often women too), so whether it was a difficult calving, or a threshing day, or additional hands to save the hay or round up cattle, neighbours helped each other and were helped in return. Some kept an informal record so the loan of a horse for a day might be repaid with three days' labour from the neighbour. My maternal grandmother got help from a neighbour with washing eggs and cleaning the house on a regular basis, and her payment was in the form of eggs and milk. Money didn't change hands for neighbourly transactions, but the favour was almost always repaid.

Although the system of *meitheal* (helping each other in turn) was starting to die out somewhat when I was growing up, farmers still rallied around when needed. Our workman had his own farm where he reared cattle. He used our machinery whenever he needed it. One evening, Dad was late in from milking and after eating his tea at 9 p.m. said, 'It looks like rain, I think I'll go and give Tommy a hand with those bales.' I knew by my mum's reaction she thought he needed a rest rather than more work, as he'd had a busy week too. I went along and when we entered the hayfield dotted with hundreds of small square bales, dark clouds were looming and the air was almost heavy with the promise of thundery rain. Tommy and another man were stacking the bales, putting two side by side and building another six on top so the stacks stood four bales high, and then securing torn fertiliser bags in under the twines of the top bales to protect them somewhat against the promised rain. There wasn't time for chat. Tommy looked over and gave Dad a nod of acknowledgement and so we set to work. Ninety minutes later and we were finished before the rain started. There was time for a quick chat before heading home for bed. Farmers are often men of few words but I knew by Tommy's nod that the help was hugely appreciated.

When I was about ten years old, Dad bought a baler and a hay turner. We started making some hay of our own, our workman borrowed it to make his hay and we did a little bit of contract work, making hay for elderly neighbours. Going to John and Kate's to make hay was another highlight of our holidays. With little road frontage, the fields stretched back one behind the other and as we went in further from field to field, it seemed like we were going back in time as it was a less intensive, more organic way of farming. Hedgerows were coppiced, grasses were native with wildflowers appearing, and it was a haven for birds and wildlife. Hay making was always a tense time, as you needed a run of at least four or five days to ensure the hay was fully dry before baling. A shower of rain just before raking the strewn hay into swathes or just before baling it set the process back by a few days as well as lowering the quality of the forage.

We had picnics in the hayfield, we jumped over swathes of hay, we watched for clouds whenever there was a breakdown – which didn't help people's nerves – we ran obstacle courses, we pulled bales into position beside stacks for an adult to lift them higher, we rode in the transport box and on top of the hay trailer going back to the hayshed, we went into their house for tea and at the end of it all, we were each handed a crisp £10 or £20 for our help. We felt as rich as kings.

Dad used to deliver sticks to a couple of elderly neighbours, chopped small enough to fit into their ranges, and always delivered in good time for Christmas. Sometimes we give neighbours a tree if one falls during a storm, but they have to saw and chop it themselves. The reason for that is farming is busier now and, in the absence of a workman, it's hard to find time to get those extra jobs done.

Do farming neighbours still help each other? Of course they do. They lend each other machinery; we borrow a bale trailer from a neighbour for a week every summer. A neighbour rang recently to say he had heard our cattle bawling, and was letting us know just in case dogs were chasing them. Another neighbour called in to check if Brian knew that a water trough in a field was losing water. He did, he had the part on the tractor and hadn't had a chance to fix it, but the friendly alert was appreciated.

A non-farming neighbour called up to tell us, early one morning, that our cattle at the outfarm were out and 'all over the place'. When we went over, we discovered the gate, which was the only new gate over there, had been stolen during the night and as dawn came and the cattle realised the gateway was open, they decided to meander up the road. As we drove in search of them, we found another neighbour looking anxious but doing his best to keep the cattle corralled in one part of the road. He was hugely relieved to see us and offered to help get them back to the field.

The vast majority of our neighbours have always lived in rural locations. They know what happens seasonally – that a couple of days of smelly slurry follow the cutting of the silage and that's just the way it works. They know we avoid doing non-essential working on Sundays and bank holidays if at all possible, so if we are working on a Sunday and interrupting their peace and quiet, there's a good reason for it – usually that the weather is going to break the next day.

Some farmers aren't so lucky. I've heard of anti-farming protestors storming into marts to disrupt proceedings. Some farmers receive complaints from neighbours about their animals mating in the field next to their garden – plus, can they stop the sheep bleating, can the cows stop staring into their garden and so on? It must be so infuriating, as that's what animals do in the normal course of life. Thankfully, our neighbours are sensible and obliging folk.

When dogs spooked some bullocks so much that one escaped into the next field – a huge corn field – the neighbour helped us to get the flighty beast out. It wasn't an easy task, as the animal was so spooked that we couldn't risk bringing in one of our dogs in case he became more frightened. An animal will normally calm down if other animals are let in with them, but we didn't want to do that because of the corn. We were just debating if we should go home and get a couple of matronly cows when he jumped over a ditch and out into the road. He went into another neighbour's yard and they corralled him in a shed, brought out their Jeep and trailer and loaded him up so he could be transported the three hundred yards to our shed in a safe and controlled manner. Sometimes we wonder why farming is so time consuming: yet when we calculated how long retrieving that single bullock took, it was about four hours. Thankfully, such incidents are few and far between.

Rural people help each other so much in times of need; the most common example is when there is a bereavement in a family. People will bring sandwiches and cake to the wake, they stay to wash up, they help with farm work, they act as car park attendants at the funeral and someone usually stays in the house in case of a burglary during the services too.

The exchange of help may not happen as frequently as it once did, but whether it's a broken-down loader, escaped livestock or community watch, farmers make good neighbours. They may not like to impose on each other's time as much as they once did, knowing that labour is often short, but they do make time for each other if help is needed.

Meeting at marts, the creamery or at community events is hugely important. Our creamery is only a mile away from the farm and we pass it daily on the way to the outfarm, so it's very convenient. I'm often surprised at how busy it is, considering we live in such a rural area. There were plans to close it a few years ago, but luckily this didn't happen. Castlecomer creamery, which is five miles away, was rebuilt on a new site and transformed into a 'country store'. No longer would men be hanging around in their dirty wellies, having a chat with other farmers or a cup of tea with the sales

238

staff when they all had their tea break. This new creamery is sparkling, but the front shop space is more suited to someone looking for tasteful garden plants than farmers picking up their supplies. A public protest, coupled with the fact that Crettyard creamery became much more profitable once the Castlecomer one moved, meant our creamery stayed open. And here farmers can stand around and chat as they wait their turn in line. It's more than a store; it's a place for farmers to catch up on the news, be it commentary on the weather, how the calving or lambing is going, whether cattle are out at grass yet and all the other subjects that make a difference to the day of a farmer.

The creamery is even more important now than half a century ago, as farmers aren't getting together for threshing days or to help each other occasionally. It's a place for farmers to get to chat for ten or fifteen minutes while they are working, or feeling they are working. It has that element of the unknown too – after all, who knows who you might meet down there.

We live a very isolated life during the calving season and are perfectly happy with that.

One day last May, I had to get bread, chocolate and petrol for the lawnmower from the local shop and a few things from the creamery. It was shopping that would normally take ten minutes. Yet I was gone for over an hour. I met three farming neighbours in the creamery, so we caught up on the successes and failures of the calving season, the breeding season and the silage harvesting.

One neighbour wanted to buy two of our bull calves as future breeding bulls – so I suppose I could claim I was also working. On going to the shop, I met two more neighbours

I hadn't seen in months and we exchanged updates on our children's progress and other news.

And I admit it, I did exactly what Brian would have done. I came home and complained about being delayed for so long – even though I had thoroughly enjoyed all the conversations.

23

THE JOY OF FARMING

Do we ever hanker after our city lives, when we worked nine to five, when we were lucky to live close to our workplaces, when we had good holidays and weekends off, when the money we earned was all ours? In farming, money disappears, the farm always seems to need continual investment and time off is a rarity.

I'd be lying if I said I never missed our walks in the New Forest on a Sunday afternoon, the anonymity of living abroad or the freedom to move house frequently. I do move furniture around a lot and, yes, farm buildings continually seem to come before my new kitchen. Yet being our own boss, working together as a family and seeing our children have an idyllic childhood means an awful lot.

We've been farming at Garrendenny now for fifteen years. We've achieved a reasonable amount on the farm during that time: we've bought land, we've expanded cow numbers and increased output; we've invested in infrastructure like new sheds, more water troughs and better cow tracks; we've embraced some of the latest developments in technology – and yet there is still a lot to do. We're very conscious that our working lives here will end in another fifteen years or so, and we know there's a lot to pack into that time. We know, too, what we want to achieve and recognise that we usually enjoy the journey much more than achieving the goal.

There are many special moments in farming and long may they continue: every morning when Lou jumps up enthusiastically to be patted and runs to discover what work the day holds; when the cows and cattle go to grass for the first time each spring; when we have a good harvest of silage; when the cows are ambling in to be milked on a fine summer's evening; when the only noises to be heard are the lowing of cattle and birdsong; when one of our favourite cows has a heifer calf; when we see a red sunset and know the sun will be shining brightly the next day.

24

RECIPES

1. SPOTTED DICK FRUIT BREAD

INGREDIENTS
- 455g plain flour
- 2 level teaspoons cream of tartar
- 85g sugar
- 1 level teaspoon baking soda
- 85g margarine or butter (butter is better for you and makes a nicer bread)
- 110g sultanas or raisins (don't use currants, they are too hard and dry when baked)
- 1 egg
- About 300ml buttermilk (quantity can vary according to the room temperature and the soakage of the flour)

METHOD
- Mix all the dry ingredients together (except the fruit).
- Add the butter in cubes and mix in with your fingertips until it looks like breadcrumbs. If the butter is at room temperature, it makes it much easier.
- Add the fruit and stir.
- Add in the beaten egg.

- Pour in some buttermilk a little at a time and mix with a broad knife until it all comes together. It should look like a dough but not be too wet.
- Turn onto your floured table and knead a little. Shape it into a round and place in a greased, floured tin. Make a vertical and a horizontal slash through the centre for a cross. Bake at 180°C for 40 to 45 minutes. To check it is baked through, tap the underside and it should sound hollow.
- Cool on a wire tray and wrap in a clean tea towel to give it a soft crust.

2. CLOTTED CREAM

WHAT YOU NEED
- Up to two gallons of raw milk
- Thermometer
- Deep roasting dish
- A day of your time!

METHOD
- If you have access to raw milk, take about a gallon and a half of milk straight from the jar in the milking parlour so it is still warm. Then pour it into a large roasting dish to a depth of about three inches.
- Leave for twelve hours at room temperature, cover to ensure it stays clean.
- Place the roasting dish over two hob rings on a very gentle heat. Bring to 75°C and keep at 75°C for an hour. The slower it comes to 75°C the better the result.

- Leave it in a cool place for twelve hours. The cream comes to the top and forms a very wrinkled surface.
- Put it in the fridge to cool down for an hour before removing the cream. This makes the cream 'stiffen' slightly and makes it easier to remove from the skimmed milk underneath.
- How do you remove the cream? A huge perforated flat spoon, almost the size of a dinner plate would be ideal. I use a fish slice! But it does the job.
- Leave in the fridge until about an hour before you want to serve it.

3. BISCUIT CAKE

INGREDIENTS:
- 255g margarine or butter (butter's nicer and better for you)
- 85g sugar
- 300g / 1 pack of Rich Tea biscuits
- 255g drinking chocolate powder (I use Cadbury's drinking chocolate. Kate alters the recipe slightly and uses 200g drinking chocolate and 55g cocoa – this gives it a darker chocolate taste, which is lovely too.)
- 2 eggs

METHOD
- Melt the butter and sugar in a large saucepan until the sugar is dissolved.
- Break the biscuits into small pieces in a separate bowl while you are waiting – children often like to do this job!

- Line a one-pound cake tin with buttered greaseproof paper so the biscuit cake will be easy to remove.
- Add the drinking chocolate to the melted butter and sugar, stirring well with your wooden spoon. It will thicken and become silky and glossy in appearance. It should be hot, not quite simmering. Remove from the heat.
- Add the two beaten eggs immediately but a little at a time, stirring quickly. Take care that they don't scramble in the heat.
- Toss in the broken biscuits and stir to ensure they are all covered with the chocolate mixture. If you haven't broken them into small enough pieces, bash them with the wooden spoon for a few minutes. (It can be quite therapeutic!) We prefer a slightly drier biscuit cake so I add a few more biscuits than the recipe states.
- Put the mixture into the tin. Pack it down as tightly as you can with the spoon. If there are gaps (or if the biscuit pieces are too big) the biscuit cake will crumble when it is cut.
- Leave it in the fridge overnight to set. Turn out and cover with melted chocolate before slicing it.
- It freezes well too, so I usually making a triple-sized one in a big Pyrex dish and cut into slabs. It's not the best thing to have in the house if you're trying to lose weight.

A WORD OF WARNING

As this cake isn't baked and it contains egg, have the mixture pretty hot when adding the egg so it cooks. Add the egg slowly and whisk like mad so it doesn't scramble.

GLOSSARY

AGITATING SLURRY

Stirring slurry with a machine at speed so the thicker liquid mixes with the watery liquid to produce a runny consistency easy to spread on the land.

BUNDAGES

Clumps of briars in the middle of a field.

COLOSTRUM

Known colloquially as 'beestings', this is the mother's first milk, high in antibodies and crucial for the newborn's good health.

DAM

A calf's mother.

DRAWING CATTLE

Bringing the cattle to a specific place, such as drawing them home, usually in a cattle trailer.

HAYCOCK
Hay gathered into a large cone-shaped structure so it can be stored as winter fodder for livestock.

HEIFER
A female bovine (up to the time she has had her second calf, after which she is referred to as a cow).

LOCKED UP
When a farmer cannot sell any livestock to other farmers because the herd has been tested positive for tuberculosis.

PIGTAILS
A temporary fence stake, easy to carry and place in the ground. It has a curly top, like a pig's tail, that the wire is hooked into.

RAM
A male sheep used for breeding.

SAVAGE CUT
A heavy cut of silage.

SIRE
A calf's father.

SPRONG
A three- or four-pronged pitchfork, known in some parts of the country as a graip or grape.

STEER
A castrated male bovine, also called a bullock.

TURNIP
A turnip in Ireland is known as a swede in other countries. It's rare that what others know as turnips are sold here.

ACKNOWLEDGEMENTS

S incere thanks to: Vanessa Fox O'Loughlin and Dominic Perrem of The Rights Bureau; to Emma Hargrave and the rest of the team at Black & White Publishing; to many writing friends for your encouragement, support and friendship (you all know who you are); to farming friends for the banter; to Sally Vince for beta-reading and being such a good mentor and friend; to Alice Rowan and Cecil Mills for sharing their memories of Garrendenny; to my parents Ruby and Joe for an idyllic farm childhood; to my brother Alden and sister Daphne for all the fun times; to my children, Will and Kate, for being more wonderful than I'd ever imagined children could be; and to Brian, the love of my life, for always having the glass half full.

FURTHER READING

Arensberg, Conrad M. and Kimball, Solon T., *Family and Community in Ireland* (Harvard University Press, 1968, second edition)

Bell, Jonathan and Watson, Mervyn, *Rooted in the Soil: A History of Cottage Gardens and Allotments in Ireland since 1750* (Four Courts Press, 2012)

– *Irish Farming Life: History and Heritage* (Four Courts Press, 2014)

– *A History of Irish Farming 1750–1950* (Four Courts Press, 2009)

Bourke, Joanna, *Husbandry to Housewifery: Women, Economic Change, and Housework in Ireland 1890–1914* (Oxford University Press, 1993)

Byrne, Anne and Leonard, Madeleine, eds, *Women and Irish Society: A Sociological Reader* (Beyond the Pale Publications, 1997)

Carter, J. W. H., *Murder in the Midlands 1862–1915* (Laois Education Publishing, 2013)

Forrest, Andrew D., *Worse Could Have Happened* (Poolbeg Press, 1999)

Heverin, Aileen, *The Irish Countrywomen's Association, A History, 1910–2000* (Wolfhound Press, 2000)

O'Donnell, Liam, *The Days of the Servant Boy* (Mercier Press, 1997)

Street, A. G., *Farmer's Glory* (Faber and Faber, 1932)

Walker, Br Linus, *Beyond Slievemargy's Brow* (Leinster Press, 2001)

NOTES

1 Walker, Br Linus, *Beneath Slievermargy's Brow* (*Leinster Express*, 2001), p.114

2 *Carlow Sentinel*, 31 March 1860

3 *Walker*, p.68

4 Central Statistics Office, *Farming since the famine: Irish farm statistics 1847–1996* (Dublin, 1997), p.22

5 O'Neill, John, 'Slievemargy', *Contact* (Carlow, 1977)

6 *Nenagh Guardian*, 17 April 1965, p.11

7 *Nationalist and Leinster Times*, 19 October 1901